God's love song

HOSEA

by Dan Wells

COMPANY

God's love song
the good book guide to Hosea
© Dan Wells/The Good Book Company, 2012. Reprinted 2014, 2016.
Series Consultants: Tim Chester, Tim Thornborough,
Anne Woodcock, Carl Laferton

The Good Book Company
Tel (UK): 0333-123-0880
Tel (int): + (44) 208-942-0880
Tel: (US): 866 244 2165
Email: info@thegoodbook.co.uk

Websites
UK: www.thegoodbook.co.uk
N America: www.thegoodbook.com
Australia: www.thegoodbook.com.au
New Zealand: www.thegoodbook.co.nz

ISBN: 9781905564255

Printed in the Czech Republic

CONTENTS

introduction: good book guides

Every Bible-study group is different—yours may take place in a church building, in a home or in a cafe, on a train, over a leisurely mid-morning coffee or squashed into a 30-minute lunch break. Your group may include new Christians, mature Christians, non-Christians, mums and tots, students, businessmen or teens. That's why we've designed these *Good Book Guides* to be flexible for use in many different situations.

Our aim in each session is to uncover the meaning of a passage, and see how it fits into the "big picture" of the Bible. But that can never be the end. We also need to appropriately apply what we have discovered to our lives. Let's take a look at what is included:

⊕ **Talkabout:** Most groups need to "break the ice" at the beginning of a session, and here's the question that will do that. It's designed to get people talking around a subject that will be covered in the course of the Bible study.

⊕ **Investigate:** The Bible text for each session is broken up into manageable chunks, with questions that aim to help you understand what the passage is about. **The Leader's Guide** contains **guidance on questions**, and sometimes ⊠ additional "follow-up" questions.

⊡ **Explore more (optional):** These questions will help you connect what you have learned to other parts of the Bible, so you can begin to fit it all together like a jig-saw; or occasionally look at a part of the passage that's not dealt with in detail in the main study.

⊡ **Apply:** As you go through a Bible study, you'll keep coming across **apply** sections. These are questions to get the group discussing what the Bible teaching means in practice for you and your church. ⊡ **Getting personal** is an opportunity for you to think, plan and pray about the changes that you personally may need to make as a result of what you have learned.

⊡ **Pray:** We want to encourage prayer that is rooted in God's word—in line with His concerns, purposes and promises. So each session ends with an opportunity to review the truths and challenges highlighted by the Bible study, and turn them into prayers of request and thanksgiving.

The **Leader's Guide** and introduction provide historical background information, explanations of the Bible texts for each session, ideas for **optional extra** activities, and guidance on how best to help people uncover the truths of God's word.

why study Hosea?

Welcome to a love song, with a difference.

Love songs are everywhere. On the radio as we drive our cars; on the soundtracks of the movies we watch; in the background as we shop and eat out. And, whether we like it or not, they're often stuck in our heads and hearts.

And yet the love they describe is often a weak or helpless love. Their lyrics are full of desire leading to disappointment, and hope followed by heartbreak. The love they tell us about is often as fleeting as the time they spend in the charts.

Love songs reflect our yearning for a love that is solid and sure: a love that we can be excited about today because we know it will still be here tomorrow. And yet those same songs expose our inability to find this love, however hard and long we search for it.

The book of Hosea is a love song. It talks of romance, of allure, of first loves; and it sings of heartbreak, of unfaithfulness, of divorce. But, crucially and uniquely, its lyrics are about a love which will never fade; which will never disappoint; and which will never say: "Enough". Hosea is about the love we all want, and the love we all need.

The singer throughout Hosea is God: and the love he talks about is his own love, lavished upon his people. It's a love song that is surprising, raw, emotional, at times uncomfortable, but always compelling.

These eight studies will thrill you with the wonder of God's love, even as they challenge you with the truth about his people. And, as you read through Hosea, you'll be provided with a soundtrack for your life which truly is worth singing along to.

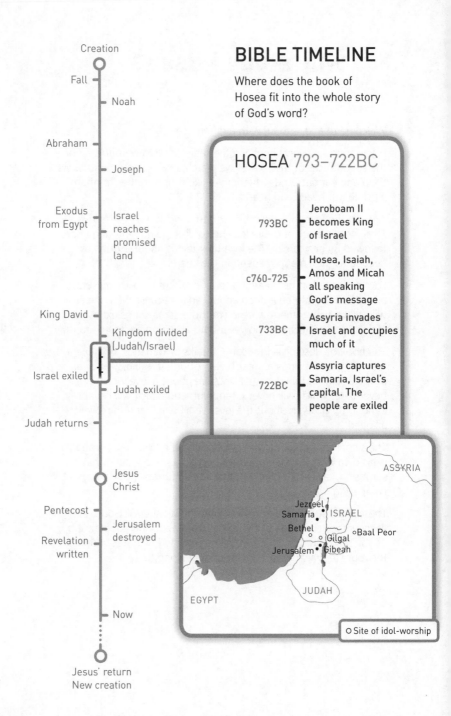

BIBLE TIMELINE

Where does the book of
Hosea fit into the whole story
of God's word?

Creation
Fall
Noah
Abraham
Joseph
Exodus
from Egypt
Israel
reaches
promised
land
King David
Kingdom divided
(Judah/Israel)
Israel exiled
Judah exiled
Judah returns
Jesus
Christ
Pentecost
Jerusalem
destroyed
Revelation
written
Now
Jesus' return
New creation

HOSEA 793–722BC

793BC	Jeroboam II becomes King of Israel
c760-725	Hosea, Isaiah, Amos and Micah all speaking God's message
733BC	Assyria invades Israel and occupies much of it
722BC	Assyria captures Samaria, Israel's capital. The people are exiled

ASSYRIA
Jezreel
Samaria   ISRAEL
Bethel
Gilgal   Baal Peor
Jerusalem   Gibeah
JUDAH
EGYPT

O Site of idol-worship

1 Hosea 1 v 1 – 2 v 1
"UNFAITHFUL"

The story so far

God speaks to Hosea, and through Hosea, during a difficult time for God's people. They have split into two kingdoms, following rival kings—"Israel" in the north, and "Judah" in the south. They enjoy neither the peace nor the prosperity that they did under their greatest kings, David and Solomon, 250 years before. Hosea lives in, and speaks mainly to, the larger northern kingdom of Israel, whose capital is Samaria.

⊕ talkabout

1. If you stopped someone in the street and asked them what sin was, how might they respond? How might the response be different if you asked someone coming out of church on a Sunday?

⊕ investigate

> **Read Hosea 1 v 1-3**

2. What is so surprising and shocking about what God asks Hosea to do?

DICTIONARY

This land (v 2): meaning everyone who lives in the land of Israel.
Conceived (v 3): became pregnant.

3. Why does God tell Hosea to do this?

• How might you expect Hosea to react? How does he respond?

4. What do these verses tell us about the state of God's people at this time?

⊡ **explore more**

optional

This is not the only time God tells a prophet to "act out" his prophetic message.

▶ **Read Jeremiah 13 v 1-11 and Ezekiel 12 v 1-6**

What do they have to act out? What is God communicating through these actions?
Why do you think God acts in this way? Does it have any implications for how we teach the Bible today?

⊡ **apply**

5. How does what happens here illustrate the seriousness of Israel's sin?

- "There is no difference ... for all have sinned and fall short of the glory of God" (Romans 3 v 22-23). What does the start of Hosea show us about ourselves? How do you feel about this?

⊡ getting personal

Think back to your answers to Question One. Do you view sin as breaking little rules, or breaking a loving relationship? Do you find your sin as shocking as Gomer's treatment of Hosea? What difference will this description of sin make to you this week?

⊍ investigate

❯ Read verses 4-9

The wording of the descriptions of Gomer's children strongly suggest that the second and third children weren't Hosea's—someone else was the father. And yet Hosea is told to raise them as his own—and to give them very significant names. His first, "Jezreel" (v 4), was the site of a famous massacre which had been caused by people turning away from God. Unsurprisingly, these three names aren't very popular nowadays!

6. Why does God ask Hosea to give the children these names, do you think?

❯ Read 1 v 10 – 2 v 1

7. How are things turned around in these verses?

• How are God's promises here more than simply a reversal of fortunes for God's people?

8. In 1 v 10, God points his people to a "place". What will happen there?

9. **Read Mark 1 v 9-11.** Who is Jesus? How does God the Father feel about him?

• **Read Mark 15 v 33-37.** What happened to Jesus' relationship with his Father as he died on the cross?

• **Read 2 Corinthians 5 v 21** and **Galatians 3 v 26-27.** What has Jesus' death achieved for his people?

10. How is the cross the "place" God pointed his people to in Hosea 1 v 10?

➔ apply

11. Why do we need to appreciate what sin is if we are to grasp the true wonder of the cross?

▢ getting personal

Have you appreciated the fact that at the cross God forsook his Son so that he could call you "my child"—if you trust in him?
How will you allow this truth to affect your feelings towards him, and about yourself, this week?

⬆ pray

Thank God for his grace shown in the Lord Jesus, which has turned you from being "not my people" into "children of the living God"?

Spend some time **asking God** for his forgiveness for the times you have treated sin lightly and superficially. Share with the group those sins you are willing to; speak to God silently about the others.

2 "IF YOU LEAVE ME NOW"

Hosea 2 v 2 – 3 v 5

The story so far

God's told Hosea, his prophet, to marry a prostitute who then left him. This was a visual way of showing Israel that sin is spiritual adultery.

⊕ talkabout

1. Can you think of a situation where someone corrected a mistake you had made? How did they do it, and how did it make you feel?

⊕ investigate

> **Read Hosea 2 v 2-13**

2. What have God's people done (v 2)? Why do they deserve a "rebuke"?

> **DICTIONARY**
>
> **Rebuke (v 2):** firmly tell off.
> **Lovers (v 5):** an image used for the false gods Israel was worshipping.
> **Acknowledged (v 8):** realised.
> **Lewdness (v 10):** in this context, nudity.
> **Sabbath days (v 11):** the one day in each week when Israel enjoyed a day of rest, and remembered they needed to trust God to help them with their work.
> **Baals (v 13):** false gods worshipped by nations around Israel.

3. How have God's people done this to God (v 5, 8, 12-13)?

• **Read Exodus 17 v 1-7.** What has Israel forgotten about? Why does this make their actions in Hosea's time even more inexcusable and stupid?

4. How will God discipline his people? What is this discipline intended to achieve?

explore more

> **Read Ezekiel 16 v 1-19**

What does this passage tell us about the relationship between God and his people?
What has God done, and what have the people done?

optional

5. **Read Luke 15 v 11-24.** What do this parable of Jesus, and Hosea 2 v 2-13, tell us about a life lived without God?

• How should we react when we realise we've turned away from God?

⤳ apply

6. Why is it good news that God disciplines his people?

• When God disciplines us through the circumstances we face, how should we respond?

⊡ getting personal

Are there good things in your life that you have never thanked God for? Or that you use for yourself, but not to serve him?
Are you experiencing God's correction and discipline in your life today? If you are, what might God be teaching you?
Remember that while God *disciplines* his children, he does not *punish* them. All our punishment has already been taken by Jesus at the cross.

⬇ investigate

❯ **Read Hosea 2 v 14 – 3 v 5**

7. How is verse 14 a turning point?

DICTIONARY
Allure (2 v 14): seduce, woo. **Invoked (2 v 17):** appealed to for help. **Covenant (2 v 18):** binding agreement. **Betroth (2 v 19-20):** get engaged to. **Ephod (3 v 4):** something worn by priests.

• In what ways are Israel's problems turned around in these verses?

8. What would being led "into the wilderness" (v 14) have reminded Israel of? (Exodus 19 v 1-8 may help you.)

Verses 19 and 20 use the language of a dowry or "bride price". This was the money that a groom's family would need to pay to the bride's family in order for a marriage to go ahead.

9. What ingredients are needed in v 19 and 20 to restore this marriage? Who can provide these things?

10. What is shocking about 3 v 1?

• What is shocking about verse 2?!

- Look at what Hosea is to *do for* Gomer, and *say to* Gomer. How is this a picture of God and his people?

11. **Read 1 Peter 1 v 18-19** ("redeemed" means "bought back"). How do Hosea's actions point us towards Jesus' death?

⊖ apply

12. How was Gomer to show that she appreciated what Hosea had done for her, and had returned to live with him as his wife? What does this tell us about our relationship with God as his redeemed people?

⊡ getting personal

What value do you put upon yourself? How might that change if you thought of yourself as God's chosen bride, bought with a price? How will this change of attitude also change your actions and desires?

⊼ pray

- Spend some time **thanking God** for purchasing us as his bride through the cross.

- **Ask God** to show you where you are (or could be) thanking and loving things that are not him. Ask him to help you be faithful to him.

3 Hosea 4 – 5
"D.I.V.O.R.C.E."

The story so far

God told Hosea, his prophet, to marry a prostitute who then left him. This was a visual way of showing Israel that sin is spiritual adultery.

God promised to woo his people back to relationship with him. He'd buy them back—at the cost of his Son's life. He told Hosea to visualise this by buying his wife back so that she could live with him and enjoy his love again.

⊕ talkabout

1. Why does it matter who leads your church? What are the qualities you would most like to see in a church leader?

⊕ investigate

In verse 1 God brings a "charge" against His people, using language similar to divorce proceedings.

> **Read Hosea 4 v 1-6a**

2. What has broken the relationship between God and his people? What is the root cause (v 1, 6a)?

> **DICTIONARY**
>
> **Acknowledgement (v 1):** recognition, understanding of who someone is.

3. What effect do the actions of God's people have on God's land?

4. **Read Romans 1 v 18-20 and 28-32.** What effect does our sin have on our world today?

➔ apply

5. What reasons do people give for the world being messed up? What kind of solutions does that lead them to?

• What do Hosea 4 and Romans 1 tell us is the problem? What do they suggest is the solution?

• Why does this tend to be an unpopular answer, do you think?

Are there areas of your life where you have never really thought about how God wants you to live? Think about your work life, bank balance, relationships with family and friends, purchasing decisions, where you live… the list is endless!

Are there parts of your life in which you know what God wants, but are choosing to ignore that knowledge?

⊡ investigate

> **Read verses 6b-13**

6. Who is God singling out here?

7. What were these men supposed to be doing for God's people?

• What have they done instead?

8. How will God punish the priests? How does God's judgment of them fit their crimes?

optional

⊡ explore more

> ▶ Read Hosea 5 v 8-15

How else have God's people and their leaders acted unfaithfully?
What more do we learn about God's coming judgment on Israel?

⊡ apply

Hosea says: "Like people, like priests" (4 v 9). God's priests lead and direct God's people.

9. What does this mean for God's people today?

10. **Read Hebrews 7 v 23-27.** Who is God's high (ie: chief) priest today? Why is he a wonderful priest to have?

11. We need church leaders today who are the opposite of the priests in Hosea's day. Read through the passage again, and work out what a good church leader would look like.

- What would the mistake the priests were making in Hosea's day look like in your culture?

getting personal

Are you too eager to put your trust in an earthly leader, rather than Jesus as your High Priest?
Are you ever too slow to follow a church leader who is leading the church to be more like Jesus?
How can you encourage, support and show loyalty to good, godly leaders this week?

⬆ **pray**

Thank God that we have a perfect High Priest who meets our need in the Lord Jesus Christ.

Ask God that you would be people who continue to acknowledge God and choose to follow leaders who will help you do this wisely and boldly.

Confess any ways in which you have seen yourself in the sinfulness of the people in Hosea's day. Thank God that in Jesus he came to bring you back into loving relationship with him.

4 Hosea 6 – 7
"SORRY SEEMS TO BE THE HARDEST WORD"

The story so far

God told Hosea, his prophet, to marry a prostitute who then left him. This was a visual way of showing Israel that sin is spiritual adultery.

God promised to woo his people back to relationship with him. He'd buy them back—at the cost of his Son's life. He told Hosea to visualise this by buying his wife back so that she could live with him and enjoy his love again.

Israel had broken relationship with God. And the priests, who were supposed to lead them in obeying God, had led them in idolatry and immorality.

⊕ talkabout

1. Why *does* sorry seem to be the hardest word?

⊔ investigate

❯ Read Hosea 6 v 1-3

2. What does Israel decide to do? What is good about what they say?

> Read verses 4-10

3. Israel has just decided to return to God. What is shocking about verse 4? What is God saying about Israel's "return"?

4. Can you spot what is missing from Israel's "return" in verses 1-4?

5. Look at the description of Israel in v 7-10. Given their words in v 1-3, what is so horrible about it?

⊡ explore more

optional

> Read Hosea 7 v 3-12

What are some of the vivid pictures God uses to describe Israel? How do they show us the true state of the people's hearts?

The same sinful attitudes look different depending on the era and the culture.

What would the sins you see in these verses look like in your time and place?
Which are particularly challenging to you as a group?

6. What does God desire people to display? How does this help us understand the kind of religion he is pleased by?

➔ **apply**

7. How can we, as church members today, be like Israel was in Hosea's day?

🙂 getting personal

God is being blunt with his people here—so this box is blunt, too! Do you ever ask God for his blessings, and tell him you want him as your God, without being truly sorry for your sins or really being willing to change?

How does God's desire for a real religious attitude of heartfelt mercy, rather than a hypocritical one of outward performance, encourage you?

How does it challenge you?

⬇ investigate

During his life on earth, halfway through discussion, Jesus quoted Hosea's words here.

▶ Read Matthew 9 v 9-13

8. Why don't the Pharisees like what Jesus is doing?

• What are the attitudes of the different people around Jesus?

9. Why do the Pharisees need to learn the lesson of Hosea 6 v 6?

• How does Matthew show us what a right response to Jesus is?

⟳ apply

10. What can we learn from Hosea 6 v 1-6 and Matthew 9 v 9-13 about truly turning back to God?

11. Why, as a follower of Jesus, will we show mercy to others?

12. How can we encourage true, heart-felt repentance among our Christian friends?

• What things might we sometimes say that actually obstruct this repentance?

⊡ getting personal

When, and why, do you find it difficult to say sorry to God? When, and why, do you find it hard to show mercy to others?

Time spent confessing your sins will prompt you to say a real sorry. And it will remind you that you are a sinner in need of mercy, and so motivate you to show mercy to others.

Would it help you to decide a time each day when you will reflect on your life, and truly repent of your sins?

⊡ pray

Ask for God's forgiveness for the ways you can be religious on the outside but not repentant in your hearts.

Pray that God would work in you by his Spirit to enable you truly to say sorry to him.

Thank God for the mercy he has shown you through Jesus. Thank God for calling you to follow his Son and find true forgiveness in him.

5 Hosea 8 – 10
"REAP THE WILD WIND"

The story so far

Though Israel had committed spiritual adultery, God promised to woo his people back to relationship with him. He'd buy them back—at the cost of his Son's life. Hosea's marriage to a reformed prostitute was a picture of this.

Israel had broken relationship with God. And the priests, who were supposed to lead them in obeying God, had led them in idolatry and immorality.

God rejected Israel's fake return to him, because he knew they were not truly sorry, and did not intend to change.

⊕ talkabout

1. What's the most urgent warning you've received? How did you respond?

⊕ investigate

▶ Read Hosea 8 v 1-14

This chapter begins with a trumpet blast—a warning siren to God's people about judgment.

2. Why do Israel think that they are safe from God's judgment (v 2, 11-13)?

> **DICTIONARY**
>
> **Sow (v 7):** plant. Here, it means what people trust in to give them what they need.
> **Assyria (v 9):** a superpower to the north of Israel.
> **Oppression (v 10):** domination.
> **Altars for sin offerings (v 11):** places you could sacrifice an animal in order to have your sins forgiven.

3. What reasons does God give to show that his judgment is fair and just (v 1-3, 11-14)?

(⊡) **explore more**

optional

▶ **Read Hosea 9 v 1-9**

How will God's judgment put an end to Israel's superficial religion? How do these verses expose Israel's attitude to God and his word?

God tells Israel they are acting as they did "in the days of Gibeah" (v 9). He's referring to a notorious moment in Israel's history, from the time of the judges around five centuries before...

▶ **Read Judges 19 v 11-30**

What is God saying about Israel in Hosea's day? How do you think you'd react if God said this about you, or your church?

In Hosea 8 v 7, God accuses Israel of sowing the wind—pursuing things which are empty and worthless.

4. What worthless things has Israel gone after (v 4-6, 8-10)?

• How does God describe his judgment of these things (v 7a)? What does this tell us about the nature of his judgment?

→ apply

5. How do people who are outwardly religious "sow the wind" today?

⊡ getting personal

What makes you feel safe from God's judgment? Are you trusting in your own deeds, religious activities or moral achievement? Or do you recognise your sin and simply come to God for undeserved mercy?

↓ investigate

❯ Read Hosea 10 v 5-8 and 12-15

6. What is coming to Israel, and why?

> **DICTIONARY**
>
> **Beth Aven (v 5):** "house of wickedness": God's name for the place Israel kept one of its idols.
> **Tribute (v 6):** an offering.
> **Samaria (v 7):** capital of Israel.
> **High places (v 8):** idol-worshipping sites were often on mountaintops.
> **Reap (v 12):** gather (a harvest).
> **Bethel (v 15):** ie: Israel.

7. What do the cries of the people (v 8) tell us about the judgment they face?

8. How should God's people have responded to this message of judgment (v 12-15)? What did they do instead?

And, just as God warned through Hosea, in 722 BC Assyria conquered and destroyed Israel.

9. **Read Luke 23 v 26-34.** It's AD 33(ish), and the people of Jerusalem—Israel—have decisively rejected Jesus. What future event does He warn the people about (v 30)?

And, just as God's Son warned, in AD 70 the Romans conquered and destroyed Jerusalem. God's judgment came.

• Look at Jesus' words in verse 34. Why did Jerusalem desperately need to hear, and hang on to, this?

10. **Read Revelation 6 v 12-17.** What is coming, in the future?

• How do Hosea 10 and Luke 23 warn us of the folly of ignoring this?

➔ apply

11. What effect will a correct view of God's judgment have on:

- how we see this world?

- how we speak to those who are rejecting Jesus?

- how we feel about the forgiveness we have through Jesus?

⊡ getting personal

How much do you dwell on the stark reality of God's judgment in your Bible reading, prayers and conversations with other Christians? What would help you to "weep" over the fate of those who reject Jesus, and rejoice more about what God has saved you from?

⬆ pray

Thank God that you no longer need fear his judgment because Jesus offers you forgiveness through the cross.

Ask God to help you to see sin as seriously as he does; to remember each day where this world is headed; and be motivated to sound a warning for others, pointing them to Jesus.

6 Hosea 11
"NEVER GOING TO GIVE YOU UP"

The story so far

Israel had broken relationship with God. And the priests, who were supposed to lead them in obeying God, had led them in idolatry and immorality.

God rejected Israel's fake return to him, because he knew they were not truly sorry, and did not intend to change.

God's judgment is real and dreadful. He warned of it through Hosea, and it came; and through Jesus, and it came; and He has warned us of a final day of judgment.

⊕ talkabout

1. What makes a good father in today's world?

⊕ investigate

▶ Read Hosea 11 v 1-4

2. Who does God describe as his "son" here? What is wonderful about God's fatherhood?

DICTIONARY

Baals (v 2): fake gods.
Ephraim (v 3): another way of describing God's people.
Cords/yoke (v 4): used to control an ox.

3. What is desperately sad about the way Israel responds to God's fatherhood?

In the next few verses, Hosea anticipates Israel's invasion by the nation of Assyria as judgment for their sin.

❯ Read verses 5-7

4. What do these verses tell us about God?

⊡ **explore more**

optional

❯ Read Deuteronomy 29 v 22-28

Israel in Hosea's time should have known these words.

What difference should they have made to the way they acted?

---

5. **Read Matthew 2 v 13-15.** How does Matthew compare Jesus of Nazareth to Israel in Hosea's day? What is he saying about Jesus?

6. **Read 1 Peter 2 v 21-23** and **Galatians 3 v 26-29.** What sort of Son was Jesus? Why is this great news for Christians?

➔ apply

7. How does this give us hope when we commit the sins of Hosea 11 v 2-4?

• How does this motivate us to avoid living in these ways?

▦ getting personal

Does this describe the Father God you know and enjoy obeying? What aspects of human fatherhood that you've experienced or witnessed are helpful in understanding and appreciating that through faith in Jesus, God is your Father?
Are there any aspects which might be unhelpful?

⬇ investigate

❯ **Read Hosea 11 v 8-11**

8. How are things amazingly turned around for Israel here?

9. What causes this amazing turn of events?

• In Hosea 11, we're given a privileged glimpse of the heart of God. What two priorities does he have? How do they seem to be in tension with each other?

10. **Read Romans 3 v 21-26.** How is it that God can be a just Judge *and* a forgiving Father to his people?

⊡ apply

11. These verses direct us to have a correct view of God and his character. What difference does it make if we think of God as…

   • a loving Father, but not a just Judge?

   • a just Judge, but not a loving Father?

   • a loving Father *and* a just Judge?

12. Imagine someone reads Hosea 11 and asks you what it's about. How could you use this passage to explain what Jesus offers through his life and death?

☺ getting personal

Do you need to be more excited by, grateful for, and appreciative of what God did through the cross? How will you do this?

God is both just and merciful. How will you make sure that justice and mercy dominate *your* perspective and actions this week?

⬆ pray

Thank God that Jesus lived the perfectly obedient life that you could not. Thank him that by dying on the cross, Jesus took the justice you deserve. Thank him that he has made you his children.

Ask God to help you enjoy the assurance of knowing that your Creator and Judge is your loving Father. Talk to him about areas in which you struggle to live as his children, and ask him for his help.

Hosea 12 – 13

"HISTORY REPEATING"

The story so far

God warned Israel they were facing judgment—and then rejected Israel's fake return to him. He knew they were not truly sorry, and didn't intend to change.

God's judgment is real. He warned of it through Hosea, and it came; through Jesus, and it came; and he has warned us of a final day of judgment.

God warned Israel they faced his judgment—*and* promised to be their loving Father. On the cross, Jesus took the punishment for his people's disobedience, and gave them his perfect obedience, making them children of God.

⊕ talkabout

1. What lessons have you learned from your past?

⊥ investigate

> **Read Hosea 12 v 1-9 and 13 v 1-3**

2. Who does Hosea compare Israel to? What does 12 v 3-4a suggest he trusted in to get what he wanted?

DICTIONARY

Judah (12 v 2), Ephraim (12 v 8; 13 v 1): names for God's people.
Defraud (v 7): cheat, steal.
Iniquity (v 8): wrongdoing.
Chaff (13 v 3): leftover bits of grain that are very light.

3. What is Israel trusting in for safety and security (v 1b, 7–8, 13 v 2)?

⊡ explore more

optional

▶ **Read Genesis 27 v 1-35.**

How does this incident illustrate Jacob's character?
How are God's people acting in the same way in Hosea's time?

4. What did Jacob end up doing (12 v 4b)?

• What will it look like for Israel to learn the lesson Jacob learned (12 v 6)?

⊖ apply

5. Where do people today look for safety and security instead of God? What makes these things attractive things to rely on?

⊡ getting personal

What is the thing most likely to draw your trust and dependence away from God? What is it that most appeals to you about that source of trust?

God "has blessed us in the heavenly realms with every spiritual blessing in Christ" (Ephesians 1 v 3). Everything we need is already ours in Jesus Christ.

What do you look for in that idol? How is it deeply and lastingly already yours in Christ?

⊻ investigate

❯ Read 13 v 4-16

6.   Which events from Israel's past are highlighted here (v 4-5, 10)? What do they tell us about God and his people?

DICTIONARY

Acknowledge (v 4): recognise, accept.
Wrath (v 11): anger that is deserved.
Deliver/ransom (v 14): rescue, set free.

⊡ explore more

optional

❯ Read 1 Samuel 8 v 1-8.

Why do the people ask for a king? What is wrong with their request and how does it show the state of their hearts? How is the same attitude at work in Hosea's day?

7.   How do verses 5-6 and 9-11 show us where Israel was looking for security: and why they were foolish to do so?

8. What powerful pictures are used to describe God's judgment?

9. Why does verse 14 seem out of place in this passage?

• What can God do that neither idols (v 1) nor kings (v 10) can?

10. **Read 1 Corinthians 15 v 20-21 and 51-58.** How does God achieve the promise of Hosea 13 v 14?

⤷ apply

11. Why can Jesus give us true safety and security?

12. How should we respond to the defeat of death (1 Corinthians 15 v 58)?

• What will this look like in our everyday lives?

⊡ **getting personal**

If someone looked at your life, what evidence would show them that your safety and security are found in Jesus alone?

⬆ **pray**

Thank God that he has fully and finally defeated death through the resurrection of the Lord Jesus Christ. Thank him that because of this, all that you do in his service has eternal significance and purpose.

Ask God to work through his Spirit to show you where you are relying, or are tempted to rely, on something other than him for your safety and security. Ask him to enable you to see more of who Jesus is and what he has given you, so that you will rely on him more and more fully.

8 Hosea 14
"RETURN TO ME"

The story so far

God's judgment is real. He warned of it through Hosea, and it came; through Jesus, and it came; and he has warned us of a final day of judgment.

God warned Israel they faced his judgment—*and* promised to be their loving Father. On the cross, Jesus took the punishment for his people's disobedience, and gave them his perfect obedience, making them children of God.

Israel had decided to trust in foreign powers and their own kings for safety and security. God's judgment would show them that he alone can provide these.

⊕ talkabout

1. What would society say makes someone wise?

   • Would you personally add or change anything in that definition?

⊕ investigate

❯ Read Hosea 14 v 1-3

2. What does God tell Israel to do, and why (v 1)?

• Think back to what we have seen of Israel in Hosea's day. Why is it amazing that they have the option of doing verse 1?

3. How are Israel to return (v 2-3)?

• What does returning *to* the LORD mean turning *away* from?

• **Read 6 v 1-4.** How is the return God calls for in chapter 14 different from the one He rejected in chapter 6?

optional

⊡ explore more

▶ **Read Hebrews 13 v 15-16 and James 3 v 9-12**

What does it mean for Christians to "offer the fruit of our lips"?

➔ apply

4. How can people return to, and stay in, a relationship with God?

⊡ getting personal

The Christian life is a life of repenting—of returning to God and turning away from other things we realise we're trusting in.

Write your own prayer from Hosea 14 by filling in the gaps:
"Father, Forgive me all my sins, and receive me by your undeserved kindness, so that I can serve you.
I recognise that .... cannot save me—I will stop trusting it.I will not treat .... like a god, because it is only part of your creation. Thank you that you are my compassionate Father, and you have given me all I need. Amen."

⊡ investigate

❯ **Read verses 4-8**

5. What is life like for people who turn back to God?

6. Where does Israel's fruitfulness come from? How will they continue to be fruitful in the future?

7. How does the beginning of verse 8 interrupt the general tone of this chapter? Why does God say this here, do you think?

⊟ apply

8. How could you use verses 1-8 to explain to a non-Christian what becoming a Christian, and being a Christian, is about?

• Imagine you have a friend who has been living as a Christian, but who has now turned their back on God. How could you use these verses to encourage and challenge them?

⊡ investigate

▶ Read verse 9

9. What does it mean to be wise? What is the other option given here?

⊡ explore more

optional

▶ Read 2 Kings 17 v 7-20

How do you see the warnings from Hosea echoed in these verses? What option from Hosea 14 v 9 did Israel choose? With what result?

⊟ apply

10. Read John 15 v 5-8. How should we live as wise and fruitful Christians?

11. Think back over the book of Hosea as a whole.
  • How would you summarise its message in a sentence?

  • What have you learned, or been reminded of, about God?

  • How has it excited you about the Christian life? How has it challenged you?

⊡ getting personal

In what ways are you enjoying the blessing and fruitfulness of living in loving obedience to your Father?
Are there any ways in which you're stumbling in disobedience?
What needs to change?

⬆ pray

Thank God...

  • that he has lavished his goodness and mercy on us, calling us to be his children through the Lord Jesus Christ (1 John 3 v 1).

  • that you are able to live a truly fruitful life. Spend some time in thanksgiving for specific blessings he's given you as you've lived his way.

Ask God...

  • to make you people who continually return to him. Tell him (out loud or silently) ways in which you need to do this.

  • to help you notice when you are stumbling, and have the wisdom to change your lifestyle so that you are able to enjoy walking in his ways. Again, tell him ways in which you would like him to help you.

Leader's Guide: Hosea

INTRODUCTION

Leading a Bible study can be a bit like herding cats—everyone has a different idea of what the passage could be about, and a different line of enquiry that they want to pursue. But a good group leader is more than someone who just referees this kind of discussion. You will want to:

- correctly understand and handle the Bible passage. But also…

- encourage and train the people in your group to do this for themselves. Don't fall into the trap of spoon-feeding people by simply passing on the information in the Leader's Guide. Then…

- make sure that no Bible study is finished without everyone knowing how the passage is relevant for them. What changes do you all need to make in the light of the things you have been learning? And finally…

- encourage the group to turn all that has been learned and discussed into prayer.

Your Bible study group is unique, and you are likely to know better than anyone the capabilities, backgrounds and circumstances of the people you are leading. That's why we've designed these guides with a number of optional features. If they're a quiet bunch, you might want to spend longer on talkabout. If your time is limited, you can choose to skip explore more, or get people to look at these questions at home. Can't get enough of Bible study? Well, some studies have optional extra homework projects. As leader, you can adapt and select the material to the needs of your particular group.

So what's in the Leader's Guide? The main thing that this Leader's Guide will help you to do is to understand the major teaching points in the passage you are studying, and how to apply them. As well as guidance on the questions, the Leader's Guide for each session contains the following important sections:

THE BIG IDEA

One key sentence will give you the main point of the session. This is what you should be aiming to have fixed in people's minds as they leave the Bible study. And it's the point you need to head back towards when the discussion goes off at a tangent.

SUMMARY

An overview of the passage, including plenty of useful historical background information.

OPTIONAL EXTRA

Usually this is an introductory activity that ties in with the main theme of the Bible study, and is designed to "break the ice" at the beginning of a session. Or it may be a "homework project" that people can tackle during the week.

So let's take a look at the various different features of a Good Book Guide:

⊕ talkabout

Each session kicks off with a discussion question, based on the group's opinions or experiences. It's designed to get people talking and thinking in a general way about the main subject of the Bible study.

⊎ investigate

The first thing you and your group need to know is what the Bible passage is about, which is the purpose of these questions. But watch out—people may come up with answers based on their experiences or teaching they have heard in the past, without referring to the passage at all. It's amazing how often we can get through a Bible study without actually looking at the Bible! If you're stuck for an answer, the Leader's Guide contains guidance on questions. These are the answers to direct your group to. This information isn't meant to be read out to people—ideally, you want them to discover these answers from the Bible for themselves. Sometimes there are optional follow-up questions (see ⊻ in guidance on questions) to help you help your group get to the answer.

⊡ explore more

These questions generally point people to other relevant parts of the Bible. They are useful for helping your group to see how the passage fits into the "big picture" of the whole Bible. These sections are OPTIONAL—only use them if you have time. Remember that it's better to finish in good time having really grasped one big thing from the passage, than to try and cram everything in.

⇥ apply

We want to encourage you to spend more time working at application—too often, it is simply tacked on at the end. In the Good Book Guides, apply sections are mixed in with the investigate sections of the study. We hope that people will realise that application is not just an optional extra, but rather, the whole purpose of studying the

Bible. We do Bible study so that our lives can be changed by what we hear from God's word. If you skip the application, the Bible study hasn't achieved its purpose.

These questions draw out practical lessons that we can all learn from the Bible passage. You can review what has been learned so far, and think about practical differences that this should make in our churches and our lives. The group gets the opportunity to talk about what they personally have learned.

⊡ getting personal

These can be done at home, but it is well worth allowing a few moments of quiet reflection during the study for each person to think and pray about specific changes they need to make in their own lives. Why not have a time for reporting back at the beginning of the following session, so that everyone can be encouraged and challenged by one another to make application a priority?

⬆ pray

In Acts 4 v 25-30 the first Christians quoted Psalm 2 as they prayed in response to the persecution of the apostles by the Jewish religious leaders. Today however, it's not as common for Christians to base prayers on the truths of God's word as it once was. As a result, our prayers tend to be weak, superficial and self-centred rather than bold, visionary and God-centred.

The prayer section is based on what has been learned from the Bible passage. How different our prayer times would be if we were genuinely responding to what God has said to us through his word.

1 Hosea 1 v 1 – 2 v 1
"UNFAITHFUL"

THE BIG IDEA
Sin is serious: it is spiritual adultery.

SUMMARY
Unlike most of the rest of the book, this first chapter or so of Hosea is narrative, explaining God's command to Hosea to marry Gomer and the consequences of that marriage. The first two verses of chapter one introduce Hosea and the times in which he lived and prophesied. Hosea spoke mainly to the northern kingdom of Israel in the years running up to their conquest by Assyria in 722 BC.

Verses 2 and 3 then detail the command that God gives to Hosea to marry Gomer. Hosea's marriage is to be a living illustration of the unfaithfulness and infidelity that God's people have shown to God himself. It is unclear from the wording whether Gomer is already sexually promiscuous (some commentators have even suggested she might have been a prostitute) or whether God knew beforehand that she would be unfaithful to Hosea. Either way, Gomer's breaking of her marriage vows will mirror the way God's people have turned to idols.

The illustration is further developed in the naming of Gomer's three children. "Jezreel" brings to mind the ungodliness of Ahab and Jezebel and their son Joram, and Joram and Jezebel's murder at the hands of Jehu (2 Kings 9). "Lo-Ruhamah" reflects God's judgment of no longer showing love and mercy to Israel. "Lo-Ammi" demonstrates that the covenant has been broken by Israel, so they are no longer God's people.

But there is a ray of hope at the end of the chapter. Purely through God's grace, and not because of Israel's goodness or repentance, God promises to turn around his judgment and once again restore his people. As Christian believers we now understand that this reversal is achieved through Jesus' death on the cross, where God's Son, Jesus, was forsaken by his Father so that we could become his children.

Note: This session deals with adultery: both Gomer's physically, and ours spiritually. Be aware that many people carry the scars of adultery (including the adulterer), often secretly.

OPTIONAL EXTRA
The title of each session in this Good Book Guide is the title of a real song. This first one is by Rihanna. While most of her songs are not ones Christians would want to listen to or watch the videos for, this one is a helpful way to introduce or conclude this session. You can find the video at: http://www.youtube.com/watch?v=rp4UwPZfRis&ob=av3e, though do check it is appropriate for you and your group first—if not, simply play the song. Alternatively, watch the scene towards the end of Love Actually (at 1:50:10 – 1:51:27), where Karen, the character played by Emma Thompson, confronts her husband about his affair, discovered because he bought the other woman a necklace as a Christmas present. How does each of them react to the discovery and betrayal? Is Karen a fool for staying with her husband?

GUIDANCE FOR QUESTIONS
1. If you stopped someone in the street and asked them what sin was, how

might they respond? How might the response be different if you asked someone coming out of church on a Sunday? Any answer to this is a good answer! The idea is to draw out the many different ideas about sin we have—outside and inside the church. You might like to refer back to these once we've seen God's definition of sin in Hosea 1 v 1-3 (perhaps as you answer Q5).

2. What is so surprising and shocking about what God asks Hosea to do? God tells him to marry Gomer, a "promiscuous woman", an "adulterous wife". It is unclear from the text whether this means Gomer was known to be unfaithful before Hosea married her (you may want to have a discussion about what we can and can't know from these few verses). However, it is clear that God knows how Gomer will act toward Hosea when he directs Hosea to marry her.

3. Why does God tell Hosea to do this? The marriage of Gomer and Hosea will illustrate the unfaithfulness of God's people toward God Himself.

• **How might you expect Hosea to react? How does he respond?** I would have been very tempted to say "no"—or at least to ask if there will be a happy ending. Amazingly, Hosea responds in obedience to God's word and marries Gomer as God has commanded.

4. What do these verses tell us about the state of God's people at this time? They are "guilty of unfaithfulness" (v 2) because they have departed from the LORD. Though they are Israel—God's people, living in God's land—they are not living with him as God.

EXPLORE MORE
Read Jeremiah 13 v 1-11 and Ezekiel 12 v 1-6. What do they have to act out? Jeremiah is to buy a linen belt and wear it (v 1). Then he's to hide it among some rocks (v 4). Then he has to go and get it back (v 7), by which time it's useless. Ezekiel has to pack up (v 3) and walk off as though he's been exiled from his house and land (v 6). **What is God communicating through these actions?** Through Jeremiah, He's saying that, though He had treated Judah like a belt—close to Him, bound up with Him—because of their sin they are now useless, and He'll "take them off". Ezekiel's actions are an enacting of going into exile—which is what the whole of God's people face due to their rebellion. **Why do you think God acts in this way? Does it have any implications for how we teach the Bible today?** It increases the impact of their messages (as does Hosea's marriage to Gomer). You might like to discuss the implications for our styles of teaching today—clearly it show us that not all Bible teaching needs to be solely verbal!

5. APPLY: How does what happens here illustrate the seriousness of Israel's sin? These verses vividly portray sin as breaking the relationship between us and the God who made us. This is certainly not all the Bible has to say about the nature of sin, but it is an important aspect which we miss when we see sin only as breaking rules. The seriousness with which we view marital unfaithfulness should give us an insight into the deeper seriousness of sin. Although our circumstances are different from Israel in Hosea's day we are still guilty of the same unfaithfulness toward God.

• **"There is no difference ... for all have sinned and fall short of the glory of**

God" (Romans 3 v 22-23). **What does the start of Hosea show us about ourselves? How do you feel about this?** Our sin is the same as Israel's sin—it is spiritual adultery. Whenever we reject the ways of our loving Creator, we're cheating on him (because we're worshipping something else—be it ourselves, money, family, or career—in his place). Allow your group to share their feelings (which may range from not wanting to accept this, to surprise, to shame, and so on). Be careful not to let the group start excusing and down-playing each other's sin (eg: "It is very hard these days, though, isn't it?" or "Everyone does it" or "You're not that bad").

6. Why does God ask Hosea to give the children these names, do you think? They act as a reminder, both to Hosea and the people, of their unfaithfulness and God's judgment on them. Not only were their names an "acting out" of God's pronouncement of judgment, but as Hosea's family lived in the midst of Israel, so everyone was reminded of God's judgment through their names.

7. How are things turned around in these verses? Each of the judgments shown by the names of the three children are turned around in these final verses. Those who are "not my people" are called "my people" again and those who were pronounced "not loved" will be called "my loved one" once more (2 v 1). Jezreel, instead of being a byword of ungodliness, will be for ever remembered in connection with God's rescue and rule (v 11).

• **How are God's promises here more than simply a reversal of fortunes for God's people?** They are not only a

reversal of judgment, but a demonstration of God's grace and generosity. Israel will not become simply "my people" again, but will instead be called "children of the living God". Jezreel will not be removed as a byword of sinfulness but turned into a byword for God's great salvation, reuniting his people as one.

8. In 1 v 10, God points his people to a "place". What will happen there? God will say to Israel (his people): You are "not my people" and also say to them: You are "children of the living God". The tenses are quite complicated here—God seems to be pointing to a future place where he will both reject his people decisively, and accept his people as his children. If someone says this is a contradiction, then freely admit that it does seem to be! And go on to Q9…

9. Read Mark 1 v 9-11. Who is Jesus? How does God the Father feel about him? The Son of God, who God the Father loves and is completely pleased with.

• **Read Mark 15 v 33-37. What happened to Jesus' relationship with His Father as He died on the cross?** As he died, Jesus was "forsaken"—abandoned, rejected—by his Father.

⌄

• **Given what we saw about Jesus in Mark 1, why is this an astonishing thing for God the Father to do?**

• **Read 2 Corinthians 5 v 21 and Galatians 3 v 26-27. What has Jesus' death achieved for his people?** *2 Corinthians 5 v 21:* Though he was perfect (God was "well pleased" with Him, Mark 1 v 11), Jesus became "sin for us". He was treated as we deserve to be, so that "in him"—by believing in him—people can be made right with God. He became a spiritual adulterer in our place… *Galatians 3 v 26-27:* Which means that we can enjoy the relationship he deserves with his Father—through faith in him, we are children of God. So at the cross, Jesus has taken our sin on himself and has given us his relationship with God.

10. How is the cross the "place" God pointed his people to in Hosea 1 v 10? Jesus was a man, and a member of God's people, Israel. At the cross, God said to a representative of his people, who was also his Son: *You are not my people, not in relationship with me; You are suffering the pain of exclusion from my presence and love.* So the cross is also the place where God says to his people, spiritually adulterous though we are: *Your sin has been taken and dealt with, and I now call you not only my*

people, but my sons and daughters. What seems like a contradiction in Hosea 1 v 10 is in fact the two sides of the same event and place: the death of God's Son on the cross, in our place, to give us his sonship.

11. APPLY: Why do we need to appreciate what sin is if we are to grasp the true wonder of the cross? If we don't understand how serious our sin is, we'll never appreciate what Jesus went through on the cross. We'll never enjoy the status of God's children he's given us. And we'll never really thank him for willingly, voluntarily going through all we deserve. It's only as we appreciate just how serious sin is, and just how sinful we are, that we'll really be able to grasp how amazing it is that the Son of God was prepared to suffer and die in our place, and how amazing it is that we are now sons of God ourselves. Wow!

2 Hosea 2 v 2 – 3 v 5
"IF YOU LEAVE ME NOW"

THE BIG IDEA
God disciplines his people to show them they need him; and God buys pays a price to buy them back, so they can enjoy being in relationship with him.

SUMMARY
Hosea's marriage, chapter one showed us, is a picture of the unfaithfulness of God's people toward God. In chapter two, God now speaks through Hosea to explain the ways in which Israel has acted like an adulterous wife.

Verses 2 to 13 portray the picture in vivid

language, using the image of adultery to describe Israel's attitude towards God. God's people have not stayed faithful to him, but have chased after and loved other gods ("lovers", v 5, 7, 10, 12, 13). In particular, they have worshipped the Baals, who were fertility gods of the land of Canaan. They gave thanks to these other gods for the things God himself had given them (grain, new wine, oil, wool, linen, silver, gold: v 5 and v 8). And so God pronounces judgment on the people, taking away the good things he has given, so that they would know they came from his hands, not from idols.

God promises to make Israel like a desert (v 3) and to block the people's path with thornbushes (v 6).

God disciplines his people—but he does it not to punish them so much as to convince them to stop being adulterous and unfaithful and to return to him. Their return should be genuine repentance and a return to a relationship with their first love (v 7).

So there is a tremendous turnaround from 2 v 14, as God acts to seduce or "allure" Israel back. "The wilderness" is a place of testing, but also where God brought his people after rescuing them from Egypt. God is bringing them back to the place of their honeymoon.

God promises to remove the idols and false gods, and restore his relationship with his people. The language of verses 19 and 20 echo the idea of a dowry or "bride price"; God will buy back his people, at a cost.

This stage of the relationship between God and his people is pictured, again, by Hosea's marriage to Gomer. He goes and loves her again, even though he pays a high price (her unfaithfulness has clearly left her in some kind of slavery).

Ultimately, Hosea's actions point us forward to the way in which God will bring his people back, at the price of his own Son. We are "redeemed"—bought back—not with precious stones or gold, but with Jesus' blood. Like Gomer, we are redeemed to live with and love and enjoy our husband—God.

GUIDANCE FOR QUESTIONS

1. Can you think of a situation where someone corrected a mistake you had made? How did they do it, and how did it make you feel? This question is not meant as a time to confess all of our mistakes! It's an opportunity to introduce the theme of how we receive, and act on, correction from others. Highlight any stories people share where the criticism came from a desire to help, rather than to tear down.

2. What have God's people done (v 2)? Why do they deserve a "rebuke"? God's rebuke might seem harsh at first, but God's people have earned God's correction. They have been unfaithful to God and turned away to worship other gods. Hosea refers to these other gods as "lovers" (v 5), comparing their rejection of God to a wife committing adultery against her husband. The indictment in verse 13 is that Israel went after the Baals, but forgot the LORD their God.

3. How have God's people done this to God (v 5, 8, 12-13)? One of the key things Israel has done is to praise and thank other gods, especially Baal, for the things that God has given to them. In fact, every good thing comes from God (see James 1 v 17), yet the people of God believed that their food and drink, wool, linen, oil, silver and gold had all come from Baal (v 5) instead of God (v 8). They even used the things given to them by God to worship these false gods (v 12-13).

• **Read Exodus 17 v 1-7. What has Israel forgotten about? Why does this make their actions in Hosea's time even more inexcusable and stupid?** Israel had seen God's miraculous power at various points in their history (Exodus 17 v 1-7), they knew he keeps his promises and provides for his people, yet still they failed to trust him or acknowledge that their good things came from him.

4. How will God discipline his people? What is this discipline intended to achieve? God promises to take away the good things—food, drink and clothing—that he had provided, leaving his people naked and thirsty, exposing their sin of trusting false gods. God's actions are not only punishment for the people's unfaithfulness, but are intended to draw them back to God in repentance. The aim of all of God's actions is that Israel would "remove the adulterous look from her face" (v 2).

☑

- **Why does God promise to "block her path" and "wall her in" (v 6-7), do you think? How might this be a kindness?** This action of God seems unpleasant and restrictive. But the intention is that Israel would be unable to pursue other gods, and therefore would return to God, who gives them all good things. This is, in fact, a kindness (like grounding a teenager to stop them hanging out with friends who commit crimes).
- **What will removing the grain, wine, wool and linen (v 9) achieve?** God's restriction of food and clothing is aimed at exposing the people's sin of spiritual adultery and enabling them to see that it was God, not Baal, who had provided all these good things in the first place.

EXPLORE MORE
Read Ezekiel 16 v 1-19. What does this passage tell us about the relationship between God and his people? Like Hosea, Ezekiel describes the relationship of God to his people in terms of a marriage. **What has God done and what did the people do?** Ezekiel particularly highlights God's initiative in saving and rescuing his people, and the appalling nature of spiritual adultery as God's people turn away to worship other gods, giving to them the good things that God has provided.

5. Read Luke 15 v 11-24. What do this parable of Jesus, and Hosea 2 v 2-13, tell us about a life lived without God? Both expose the folly of trusting in anything other than the living God. That life seems to be free and pleasurable on the surface, but leads to disappointment, disgrace and ruin. In both circumstances, the people involved come to their senses and recognise that they were much better off before turning away.

- **How should we react when we realise we've turned away from God?** The right response to God's discipline is humble repentance, turning back to the God who is lavishly generous.

6. APPLY: Why is it good news that God disciplines his people? Discipline never sounds like a good thing, but God's discipline is intended to bring his people back to him and stop them from wandering away. It is, therefore, a very good thing that God exercises discipline, to ensure that we keep trusting and following him. In fact, Hebrews 12 v 5-11 reminds us that God's discipline means he is treating us as his children, which should give us great encouragement.

- **When God disciplines us, through the circumstances we face, how should we respond?** As we think about God's discipline, it is vital to distinguish between discipline and punishment. As believers we need not fear God's punishment, as that has been taken fully by Jesus on the cross. Difficult, even painful, circumstances do not come as punishment from God, but can be used by him to correct us and draw us closer to him, in trust and dependence. "In all things God works for the good of those who love him" (Romans 8 v 28). He may be using the circumstance we face to stop us wandering away from him.

7. How is verse 14 a turning point? God intends to restore his relationship with his people ("you will call me 'my husband'", v 16), with God wooing them and removing the adulterous worship of false gods.

- **How are Israel's problems turned around in these verses?** There is the promise of a renewed relationship between God's people, removing conflict (v 18) and a restored relationship with the land, which will again produce good things for them to enjoy. God illustrates this turn around by reversing the meaning of a number of names: "Achor" (v 15) means trouble, but God will turn it into "door of hope" (see Joshua 7); "Jezreel" was a byword for ungodliness and bloodshed, but means "God plants" and will return to that meaning as the land becomes fruitful once again (v 22). God even reverses the names of Hosea's children to demonstrate his grace (v 23).

8. What would being led "into the wilderness" (v 14) have reminded Israel of? (Exodus 19 v 1-8 may help you.) Though wilderness is a place of testing, it is also the place God brought his people after rescuing them from Egypt, before bringing them to the promised land. The desert was the place where God taught Israel how to live as, and enjoy being, His people. So in Hosea's day, the people of Israel would have understood v 14 to be God telling them he will bring them back to the beginning of their relationship in order to start again.

9. What ingredients are needed in v 19 and 20 to restore this marriage? Who can provide these things? The "bride price" is righteousness, justice, love, compassion and faithfulness—all characteristics of God himself. God is setting

a price only he can pay.

- **Use a table to compare how God, in the verses we've been studying, has shown each of these characteristics; and how His people have failed to display them.**

10. What is shocking about 3 v 1? God tells Hosea to go and love his wife again! He tells Hosea to do this even though she is *still*, at this point, being "loved by another".

- **What is shocking about verse 2?!** Hosea does it! He has to pay a price to get her back, and he is willing to pay it!

- **Look at what Hosea is to *do* for Gomer, and say *to* Gomer. How is this a picture of God and his people?** Israel has been utterly unfaithful to God, shown in v 1 with their desire to turn to other gods and, ludicrously, to love "raisin cakes" (probably used in idol worship, yet how sad that God's people abandon God because of a desire for cake!). Yet despite all this, "the Lᴏʀᴅ loves the Israelites" and this faithful, unwavering love will be demonstrated by Hosea's words and actions to Gomer. Although she has been unfaithful to him, he is to take her back as his wife, buying her back from her life of prostitution. This is what God will do for his people. And, just as Gomer is to live in faithful commitment to Hosea, so God calls his people to respond to his grace by living as his people, loving him alone.

11. Read 1 Peter 1 v 18-19 ("redeemed" means "bought back"). How do Hosea's actions point us towards Jesus' death? Like Gomer, we have been bought back from a life of adultery and unfaithfulness to live with and love the One who loves us.

1 Peter 1 v 18-19 reminds us that this was not achieved by silver or gold but by the blood of Jesus Christ, shed for us on the cross. This was what it cost God to bring us back into relationship with him—his own blood. It is this that allows us to stand as God's loved and forgiven children.

12. APPLY: How was Gomer to show that she appreciated what Hosea had done for her, and had returned to live with him as his wife? What does this tell us about our relationship with God as his redeemed people? The lavish grace and mercy that God gives inevitably has an effect on our lives, our attitudes and our actions. This is illustrated in Hosea's relationship with Gomer—after Hosea's words in v 2-3, Gomer would need to turn from her life of prostitution and remain

committed and faithful to her husband. This action does not earn the restored marriage with Hosea, but is a necessary part of that renewed relationship. In the same way, since we have been bought with a price through Jesus' death on the cross, we no longer belong to ourselves, doing whatever we want. Rather we belong to God, and therefore we should do what pleases and honours him, in every aspect of our lives.

⊠

- **APPLY: Read through 2 v 2-13, the description of Israel the adulteress. How would Israel have behaved if she had been faithful to God (it's the opposite each time!) What would these attitudes of faithfulness look like in our lives as God's people today?**

3 Hosea 4 – 5
"D.I.V.O.R.C.E."

THE BIG IDEA
God charges his people, and particularly his people's leaders, with breaking their relationship with him.

SUMMARY
Verse 1 of chapter four begins with God bringing a charge against his people, using the language of a lawsuit or divorce petition. The charges against God's people are numerous: lying, murder, stealing, adultery. But the root cause of all this ungodly behaviour is simple—a lack of knowledge (v 6) and no acknowledgement of God throughout the land (v 1). Without knowing God and his ways, the people go astray,

following their own desires and making their own rules. The end result is no faithfulness and no love.

This lack of acknowledgement of God has an effect not just on the actions of the people, but also on the world around them. Since God is the Creator and Sustainer of the world, how we act toward him affects the world in which we live. Sin has broken God's good creation and the effects detailed in verse 3 echo Paul's words in Romans 1 v 18-32, explaining how the wrath of God is revealed in the sinful actions of human beings.

God's charge of "lack of knowledge" is a

stinging indictment on God's people. Not only have they broken the relationship with God, but they were supposed to be a people marked by knowledge of God—his laws and his truth.

The priests were in charge of this function of Israel's life, and so it is they who are accused in verses 6-13. They should have been the ones who guarded God's law, teaching and encouraging the people to walk in God's ways. Instead they rejected God's law (v 6) and actively encouraged God's people to worship idols instead. They have become characterised not by holiness and godliness, but by an insatiable appetite for sexual immortality and drunkenness (v 10-11) and pagan idolatry (v 12-13). So God's judgment falls on both priests and people—as they have rejected Him, so God rejects them.

Chapter 5 (in Explore More) adds to the picture of an unfaithful people and disobedient leaders. God's judgment is pictured as a flood (5 v 10), moth and rot (5 v 12) and as a great lion (5 v 14). Although God in His judgment still desires His people to turn back to Himself (5 v 15), these verses point forward to the punishment of exile, which God will bring about through the conquering army of Assyria.

So what we need is a good priest, a leader who will lead us in knowing and obeying God. In Hebrews 7, we discover that Jesus is this perfect High Priest. It is Him we need to follow, trust and obey. And it is Him who our church leaders today need to point us to, and seek to be like.

OPTIONAL EXTRA

Devise a "job description" and "character description" of a Christian leader/pastor/minister. (If you have appointed a staff member recently, you may even want to.

dig out the job description, or equivalent, to compare!) Think about the essential qualities they need.

If you have time, come up with a reverse job description: what a pastor would be looking for in a congregation!

GUIDANCE FOR QUESTIONS

1. Why does it matter who leads your church? What are the qualities you would most like to see in a church leader? This is NOT an opportunity to discuss the merits and flaws of your church leadership—you might like to ban mention of him/them by name. But it is worth talking about what we look for when we appoint people to ministry positions; and what it is that we respond warmly to, or don't really notice, in those who are in leadership of our churches.

2. What has broken the relationship between God and his people? What is the root cause (v 1, 6a)? God through Hosea uses the language of lawsuits and divorce in v 1 to charge his people with breaking the relationship. The evidence is ungodliness in their behaviour, characterised by cursing, lying, murder, stealing, adultery and bloodshed, along with lack of love and faithfulness. But the root of this ungodliness is given at the end of v 1: "no acknowledgement of God in the land" and further explained in v 6: "my people are destroyed from lack of knowledge". God's people have broken their relationship with him because they failed to know God and his ways.

3. What effect do the actions of God's people have on God's land? Without knowledge of God and his laws, the people have gone their own way with disastrous consequences. Their actions have resulted in the ungodly behaviour we read of throughout chapter 4. But as God is also Creator, a broken relationship with him also breaks the relationship with the world he has created. We can see this from the moment of the curse in Genesis 3, alongside the painful effects that the sin of people has on God's world. For the people in Hosea's time, this meant the land "mourning" in famine, failing to produce food and causing both people and animals to waste away.

4. Read Romans 1 v 18-20, 28-32. What effect does our sin have on our world today? Romans 1 details the same deliberate rejection of the knowledge of God and the ungodly actions that result from it. 1 v 28 tells us that God actively gives people over to the effects of their sin and that this is part of what v 18 tells us is the wrath of God being revealed. This is seen in the wide variety of ungodly behaviour that is catalogued in these verses, which affects not only the people committing these sins, but also other people and the world around us.

5. APPLY: What reasons do people give for the world being messed up? What kind of solutions does that lead them to? There are plenty of reasons people might give for the world being so messed up: lack of education, corrupt politicians, financial inequality, greed and so on. Each one of these things will lead to a different "solution"—if our problem is lack of education, what we really need is more teachers and better schools around the world. If it is corrupt politicians, the solution could be revolution, to join protest marches, emigrate, or get actively involved in the political system.

• **What do Hosea 4 and Romans 1 tell us is the problem? What do they suggest is the solution?** Both Hosea 4 and Romans 1 point to a more fundamental problem, that we have failed to acknowledge God as our Creator and Lord. While there are plenty of good things we can do to alleviate immediate problems in this world, we all need more than anything else to turn back to the God who made us and ask for his forgiveness.

• **Why does this tend to be an unpopular answer, do you think?** Let your group come up with their own reasons. But perhaps there are two big reasons: it tells us we are part of the problem—we cannot simply point the finger at others; and it tells us we cannot be part of the solution—and we don't like to hear we can't save ourselves.

6. Who is God singling out here? The priests.

7. What were these men supposed to be doing for God's people? They should have been the ones who guarded the knowledge of God's laws and taught others to obey them. They had the responsibility of leading the people in trusting God and walking in obedience to his commands.

• **What have they done instead?** They have actively been involved in leading people astray to worship idols (v 7, 12). Rather than calling Israel to repent, they relish the sins of the people (v 8). Although they were the ones given the task of treasuring and teaching God's law, they have instead ignored it (v 6). Along with this comes a range of ungodly behaviour, including sexual immorality, idol worship (v 10) and drunkenness (v 11). They have failed to teach God's truth or to be examples of walking in God's ways. They are, in a sense, anti-priests.

8. How will God punish the priests? How does God's judgment of them fit their crime? Just as they have rejected and ignored him, so God will reject and ignore them. They "feed" on sin (v 8), so they will feed but never be full (v 10); as they have been adulterous and unfaithful to God, so they will give themselves over to prostitution; as they discarded God's knowledge, so they will worship idols of wood which cannot answer or give understanding. God's judgment not only exposes and punishes the people's sin but also mocks it for its foolishness.

EXPLORE MORE
Read Hosea 5 v 8-15. How else have God's people and their leaders acted unfaithfully? Israel (called Ephraim here) is a nation intent on pursuing idols. They show this in disobedience to God's commands. For instance, they move boundary stones (v 10). This is effectively stealing a person's land and inheritance—a sin committed even by the leaders. And when things go wrong, they don't turn to God for help, but turn to Assyria instead (v 13)—yet another example of unfaithfulness.
What more do we learn about God's coming judgment on Israel? It will come like a flood, with God described in dreadful terms as a "moth", "rot" and finally a terrible lion, tearing them to pieces and carrying them off into exile (through Assyria, the very nation they turned to for help).

9. APPLY: What does this [the fact that God's people are like God's priests] mean for God's people today? Who leads our churches (and our denominations if we are in one) matters greatly. Over time, the worship, theology and ethics of a church will come to reflect its leaders'. What a good leader is like is the subject of Q11—but if

your group go down the path of discussing what people should do if their church leader is not a godly man, let them think about this at this point for a while.

10. APPLY: Read Hebrews 7 v 23-27. Who is God's high (ie: chief) priest today? Why is he a wonderful priest to have? The priests in Hosea's time were weak and sinful, unable to lead the people as they should have. Hebrews 7 reminds us that we have a perfect, sinless High Priest in the Lord Jesus. He is a wonderful priest to have because he does not fail in the ways that Hosea's priests did. He lives for ever and offered the perfect sacrifice for our sins through his death and resurrection. Now he stands before his Father and intercedes for us, so we can know with confidence we are accepted by God.

11. APPLY: We need church leaders today who are the opposite of the priests in Hosea's day. Read through the passage again, and work out what a good church leader would look like. The leaders of God's people should have been teaching God's truth and encouraging the people to live in obedience to God's commands. As Christians we need leaders who will build up God's people in the knowledge of God, even when that is unpopular. They will teach God's truth clearly, leading us away from worshipping things that are not God. They will care about those they lead and be willing to challenge them about their sin (as well as watching out for sin in their own lives). The best leaders are not necessarily the most charismatic, dynamic or eloquent, but those who are faithful to God and his word.

• **What would the mistake the priests were making in Hosea's day look like**

in your culture? Your answers to this, of course, will depend on what country and area you live in, and what your church is like. Some suggestions:

- 4 v 6: not holding to the clear teaching of the Bible eg: on marriage, hell, financial giving, etc.
- v 8: allowing and even encouraging the sins church members most enjoy.
- v 10: sexual immorality (remember, lust is immorality even though it's in the mind).
- v 11: drunkenness or general excess.

- v 12: any idolatry. We may not bow down to a wooden stick, but church leaders are just as prone as the rest of us to idolising career, popularity, possessions, sex, and so on.
- v 14: "shrine-prostitutes" were part of the religions of nations surrounding Israel. So today, this might look like adopting some practices of other religions (including atheism, which is a belief system), or seeking to suggest that all religions are fundamentally the same.

Hosea 6 – 7

4 "SORRY SEEMS TO BE THE HARDEST WORD"

THE BIG IDEA

Returning to God and his blessings requires saying, and meaning, sorry. God can see through fake repentance.

SUMMARY

Hosea 6 v 1-3 allows us to listen in as God's people speak to one another. On the face of it what they say is good—"Let us return to the Lord"—knowing that although he has punished them, he is compassionate. They also seem to recognise that they have not acknowledged God and so vow to "press on to acknowledge him", feeling confident that he will restore their relationship.

However, Israel's seeming repentance lacks punch: they do not say sorry to God or ask for his forgiveness. Instead, they presume upon it. In v 4-10, God exposes what they are really like. Their regret is short-lived, going away quickly like the morning mist. Although they appear to be seeking God's

forgiveness, in fact their repentance is superficial. God is more interested in the state of their hearts than the words that come easily to their lips: "I desire mercy, not sacrifice" (v 6). Israel were happy to go through the motions of religious observance, offering sacrifice, but God wants to see a change in their attitudes and desires, truly going his way, not their own. Verses 7-10 shows Israel is still resolutely going away from God, even with the facade of religion and piety. Chapter 7 (looked at in Explore More) adds to the picture with a number of vivid images to describe Israel's ungodliness and lack of trust in the Lord.

Jesus picks up on the words of Hosea 6 v 6 in his dealings with the Pharisees. He tells them to "go and learn what this means…" The Pharisees, like Israel in Hosea's day, were concerned with outward appearance and looking religious. They were angry that Jesus spent so much time with undesirable outcasts and sinners. They failed to see God's mercy for undeserving sinners, and failed to see that they needed that mercy and help as much as anyone else. And, since they did not realise they needed mercy, they were not going to show it to others.

OPTIONAL EXTRA

Watch the scene from the film *Road to Perdition* where Connor (played by Daniel Craig) tries to say sorry to his father (played by Paul Newman) at a meeting. Why doesn't Connor's father accept his apology?

GUIDANCE FOR QUESTIONS

1. Why does sorry seem to be the hardest word? There will no doubt be many possible answers to this question, but most can probably be categorised into either pride ("I don't want to admit I'm wrong") or independence ("I don't want to acknowledge my debt to someone else").

2. What does Israel decide to do? What is good about what they say? On the surface this seems to be a positive turning point. God's people resolve to return to the LORD, recognising that he is the one who has brought judgment upon them. Their words seem to show them depending on his goodness and mercy, saying that they desire to "press on to acknowledge him".

3. Israel has just decided to return to God. What is shocking about verse 4? What is God saying about Israel's "return"? God's words expose Israel's love and commitment as being like "morning mist", here one moment and gone the next. Although it seems as if they have turned back to God, it is not genuine repentance. They are outwardly very religious, offering sacrifices and going through the motions,

but their hearts are still turned away from God and his commands.

4. Can you spot what is missing from Israel's "return" in v 1-4? Looking a bit more closely at their words, we see that they do not actually say sorry to God. They do not seem to acknowledge their sin and idolatry, and presume on God's mercy and grace rather than asking for it. Their repentance has many of the right words but is not accompanied by a change of lifestyle and attitude. They want the goodness of God (and for him to return the rain to produce crops) without obedience to him.

5. Look at the description of Israel in v 7-10. Given their words in v 1-3, what is so horrible about it? Israel's words and actions fail to match up: they are saying the right thing, but their deeds demonstrate something else. Verses 7-10 highlight how Israel is living—breaking the covenant and being unfaithful to God (through worship of other gods). Their towns, like Gilead, are stained with the blood of their crimes. Their actions show that their hearts are far from God, despite their repentant words.

EXPLORE MORE
Read Hosea 7 v 3-12. What are some of the vivid pictures God uses to describe Israel? How do they show us the true state of the people's hearts? They are like an oven (v 4) which the baker does not need to stir to keep going, smouldering all night and still burning strongly in the morning (v 6), burning in their case with a desire for ungodliness; they are like a mixed cake (v 8), indistinguishable from other nations and, like a flat loaf not turned over (which makes it burnt on one side and uncooked on the other), inedible and useless; like a person going grey but who is ignorant of

it (v 9); like a foolish dove (v 11, 12) flitting between two masters, Egypt and Assyria, but failing to trust God.
What would the sins you see in these verses look like in your time and place? Which are particularly challenging to you as a group? Encourage your group to be specific here. Some, such as adultery (v 4) are straightforward; others, such as compromising in order to impress authority (v 3) need more thinking about.

6. What does God desire people to display? Mercy, not sacrifice; reflecting God and his character in their actions, wanting his mercy and demonstrating that mercy toward others. God's people have been doing the opposite: concerning themselves with outward religious actions without an inner change of heart. **How does this help us understand the kind of religion he is pleased by?** The kind of religion that God delights in is one that is less concerned with ritual and ceremony and more with pleasing God throughout life.

7. APPLY: How can we, as church members today, be like Israel in Hosea's day? The same sinful tendencies that Israel displayed are no different for us today. It is all too easy to put on an outward religious veneer, but for our hearts still to be very far from God. We can say the right thing, go to church and appear very devout before other Christians. But God is much more interested in our attitude and the state of our hearts than our outward appearance to others.

8. Why don't the Pharisees like what Jesus is doing? The Pharisees saw Jesus as a rabbi and teacher (not unlike themselves). Yet Jesus was spending time with undesirable folk like "tax collectors and sinners", the very people the Pharisees

worked hard to separate themselves from. Jesus even goes as far as to call Matthew, a tax collector, to be one of his disciples! The goal of the Pharisees was to appear holy by not associating with those who appeared to be "sinners", but Jesus makes it his aim to associate with these kinds of people.

• **What are the attitudes of the different people around Jesus?** The Pharisees see themselves as holy and righteous, and are angry with Jesus for acting in a different way from what they expected. They don't see they have a problem and don't think they need Jesus' help. The tax collectors and "sinners" on the other hand know they have a problem. They recognise that they are not righteous and are separated from God, and look to Jesus for mercy and forgiveness. Both groups need Jesus' help but only one is willing to admit it.

9. Why do the Pharisees need to learn the lesson of Hosea 6 v 6? They are concentrating on outward appearance, like Israel in Hosea's time, rather than looking to show God's mercy. When Jesus quotes Hosea 6 v 6, he is telling the Pharisees that if they really knew God, they would approve of Jesus reaching out to sinners, rather than being concerned solely about appearances. Even more, they would see that they too need God's mercy and forgiveness.

• **How does Matthew show us what a right response to Jesus is?** He hears Jesus' call to follow him, and immediately leaves his previous way of life. He receives Jesus into his home, and uses the resources he has to enable Jesus to show mercy to those who desperately need it.

10. APPLY: What can we learn from Hosea 6 v 1-6 and Matthew 9 v 9-13 about truly turning back to God?

It means: recognising we need God's mercy, through Jesus' sacrificial death in our place; seeking God's desires, such as showing God's mercy through sharing the gospel, rather than being more concerned about outward appearances and superficial religious behaviour; and turning around with our hearts and actions, not just our words.

11. APPLY: Why, as a follower of Jesus, will we show mercy to others? If we understand that we need, and have been given, God's mercy—that we don't deserve anything from him, and must rely on his goodness in forgiving us—then our view of those around us will radically change. Instead of thinking they should get what they deserve (if they have wronged us, or our family, or our society) we will see them as people who we can show mercy to, as God has to us: not because they deserve it, but because we know what it is to receive and be transformed by mercy.

12. APPLY: How can we encourage true, heart-felt repentance among our Christian friends? We too need to turn back to God and ask forgiveness for the

ways we have failed to trust and honour him. We need the encouragement and help of our Christian friends to help us do that— helping us to see the idols that take our worship away from God, and how we cover this up with outward religious behaviour. This means being open and honest with each other about our need to repent; asking each other for prayer when we need it; and being willing to challenge one another.

- **What things might we sometimes say that actually obstruct this repentance?**
  - We make excuses: "It's very hard not to worry, isn't it?" or "Oh, I do that too".
  - We can suggest God's word isn't clear when it is: "Of course, Ephesians 5 v 18 only mentions wine, not beer…"
  - We can suggest sin doesn't matter: "I'm sure God understands the pressure you were under"; "It's only a little thing".
  - We can imply we can make up for our failures: "On the plus side, you did say sorry to her afterwards"; "I'm sure God's pleased you helped at that church event, even if you did snap at someone else". We often mean well—but discourage real repentance.

5 Hosea 8 – 10
"REAP THE WILD WIND"

THE BIG IDEA
God's judgment is deserved, dreadful, and very real.

SUMMARY
Chapter 8 begins with a trumpet call, a warning siren to wake up the people of Israel to the dangers of rejecting God and facing his judgment. They are in grave

danger. "An eagle", the great power Assyria, is ready to invade (as predicted in Deuteronomy 28 v 49).

The reason for this is that the people have turned away from God: broken the covenant, rebelled against God's commands (v 1), rejected what is good (v 3), made decisions for themselves and turned to idols (v 4). It is amazing that the people who God chose as his own have rejected him and turned once again to golden calves as idols, just as in the days of Moses and Aaron. This ought not to happen for those who know God, so Hosea cries out in desperation and shame: "They are from Israel!" (v 6).

The people need to realise that their actions are rebellion against the God who made them and chose them, and that those actions have dire consequences. It is described in pivotal v 7, as "they sow the wind and reap the whirlwind". Israel have sown wind—pursuing things that are empty and producing hollow unfruitfulness—and now they face the resulting whirlwind of God's judgment, delivered through the foreign army of Assyria ("whirlwind" can also be used to describe the sound of approaching chariots). Their kings will not save, their idols will be crushed and they will be swallowed up among the nations (v 8), facing invasion by the very nations they sought safety and security from.

The day is coming when the people will be driven to saying to the mountains: "Cover us" (10 v 8), preferring a rockfall to God's just punishment.

These words are picked up by Jesus, as he prophesies Jerusalem's judgment on the way to his cross—a judgment that duly came in AD 70 when the Romans destroyed the temple. And they are quoted in Revelation 6, as a promise of the judgment which is still to come.

All of which means that we desperately need to hear Jesus' words from the cross: "Father, forgive them". The reality of the awfulness of God's judgment leaves us needing, and appreciating, our forgiveness through Jesus all the more. And it should motivate us to warn others of judgment, and point them to Christ.

OPTIONAL EXTRA

Find some photos of famous mountains, and get your group to guess which they are. This links to Q7, 9 and 10—to ask a mountain to fall on top of you in order to avoid something else happening shows just how awful the alternative is.

GUIDANCE FOR QUESTIONS

1. What is the most urgent warning you have ever received? How did you respond? This introduces the idea of being warned and heeding that warning.

2. Why do Israel think that they are safe from God's judgment (v 2, 11-13)? Israel reacts to the warning of God's judgment by complaining "Our God, we acknowledge you!". They build altars and offer sacrifices (v 11, 13), having an appearance of godly behaviour and thinking that this will keep them safe from judgment.

3. What reasons does God give to show that his judgment is fair and just (v 1-3, 11-14)? God's people may say his judgment is unfair, but God demonstrates the justice of his coming judgment. He had chosen Israel as his own people, yet they had broken the covenant (much like breaking marriage vows), rebelled against his law, and rejected what is good (both God's ways and God himself). "Israel has forgotten their Maker" (v 14) and trusted in other things. So God's just and fair judgment will come upon a people who have chosen to rebel against him and his rule.

EXPLORE MORE

Read Hosea 9 v 1–9. How will God's judgment put an end to Israel's superficial religion? Despite the warning of judgment, Israel is rejoicing like the other nations. One reason for this is that their superficial religion makes them feel safe from God's judgment. As a result, God's judgment will take away their rituals and religious actions—the land will not produce food or wine for sacrifices (v 2) and the people will be removed from the God's land. They will have nowhere to offer sacrifices (v 4) and nowhere to celebrate religious festivals (v 5).

How do these verses expose Israel's attitude to God and his word? God exposes their sin and hypocrisy. All the time they are going through the motions of being religious, they have been unfaithful to God (v 1), trusting in idols and other nations. They have rejected God and have rejected his words. God's word is spoken by his prophet, but he is considered insane, and people lie in wait to ambush him before he can speak God's message (v 7, 8)!

Read Judges 19 v 11-32. What is God saying about sin in Israel's day (v 9)? It is as serious and horrific as what happened in Gibeah, where we see homosexuality, cowardice, rape and murder. "Gibeah" is shorthand for almost unthinkable sinfulness.

How do you think you'd react if God said this about you, or your church? Your group would most likely be shocked! We may (and should) listen and change; but our instinct is probably to make excuses, downplay the seriousness, or just ignore it.

4. What worthless things has Israel gone after (v 4-6, 8-10)? They have set up and put their trust in kings and princes (v 4) instead of God and the rulers he has chosen. They have gone after worship of idols which are simply man-made objects and cannot save (v 5-6). Finally, they have looked to other nations, such as Assyria, for strength and security, failing to trust God and be distinctive; instead they have been "swallowed up" by the nations around

them (v 8). Each one of these things is futile to trust in and produces no result and no protection against God's judgment.

• **How does God describe his judgment of these things (v 7a)? What does this tell us about the nature of his judgment?** He will make Israel "reap the whirlwind". That is, his judgement will fall on, and show the uselessness of, the things they have chosen to trust and worship. They will get what they have chosen. They trust Assyria—Assyria will invade them. They serve a calf-idol—this will be smashed to pieces. God judges people by handing them over to what they have chosen, to the consequences of their own decisions (see Romans 1 v 21-31). Ultimately, God judges people by giving them what they want: life for ever without him. But this will mean life without his gifts—life without anything good, in hell. Hell is where people will reap the whirlwind of what they chose—things which are just wind—in this life.

5. APPLY: How do people who are outwardly religious "sow the wind" today? This is a chance to think about what our hearts can trust in, and what we can look to to give us security and satisfaction, even as we go to church, say the right words, do the right things. There are an infinite number of ways to "sow the wind", for example: trusting career for security instead of God; seeking satisfaction in thinking sexually about people we're not married to; thinking deep down that we'll get eternal life because we are good/ religious people, rather than because Jesus has saved us from the judgment we deserve.

6. What is coming to Israel, and why? The people of Israel face the imminent threat of God's judgment through the invading army of Assyria. The Assyrians were the dominant superpower of the time, and God would use them as the instrument of his judgment on his people. The Assyrians would invade, taking away the idol as a tribute, removing the king (he'll float away like a twig) and taking the people into exile.

7. What do the cries of the people (v 8) tell us about the judgment they face? God's people will cry to the mountains and hills to fall on them and cover them. The nature of God's judgment is such that the people would rather be caught in a landslide or rockfall than face the reality of God's punishment. Perhaps they foolishly think they can hide from God if a mountain covers them up! Israel's outcry shows they viewed God's righteous wrath as something terrible.

8. How should God's people have responded to this message of judgment? What did they do instead? The urgent warning of God's judgment at the beginning of chapter 8 should have been a wake-up call to God's people to turn back to him. They had previously "sown the wind" but instead they should "sow righteousness" (v 12) by seeking the Lord. The message of God's judgment should have led the people back to the Lord. Sadly, they did not heed the warning. They chose to continue in stubbornness and rebellion, planting wickedness and depending on their own strength (v 13). So they chose to face the just and dreadful punishment of God.

9. Read Luke 23 v 26-34. It's AD 33(ish), and the people of Jerusalem—Israel—have decisively rejected Jesus. What future event does he warn the people about (v 30)? A day when they want the mountains to fall on them—which,

as we've seen from Hosea 10, is a day of God's judgment. Jesus is pointing towards AD70, when Roman armies conquered and destroyed Jerusalem (see Luke 19 v 41-44).

• **Look at Jesus' words in verse 34. Why did Jerusalem desperately need to hear, and hang on to, this?** Because they were facing dreadful judgment—they needed God's forgiveness. And as Jesus hung on his cross, he asked God to forgive people. Of course, it is through the cross that even the most hardened rebel can be forgiven, avoid judgment and be given a place in God's kingdom (see Luke 23 v 39-43). In a city under judgment, the offer of forgiveness should come as a great relief (though, in the main, it was totally ignored).

10. Read Revelation 6 v 12-17. What is coming, in the future? The ultimate day of God's judgment. The closing verses of the chapter picture the wrath of God on that day, and the reality of that dreadful day dawning on those who face God's punishment.

• **How do Hosea 10 and Luke 23 warn us of the folly of ignoring this?** God's judgment has been predicted in the past, and has then come, and been horrific. This shows us that God's judgment is real, and something to be avoided at all costs. Ignoring or downplaying it will not change the truth about what is coming.

11. APPLY: What effect will having a correct view of God's judgment have on:
• **how we see this world?** It is under judgment. We shouldn't be surprised by people rejecting God, or by the world going "wrong". We shouldn't be too attached to what this world offers. We must ensure we don't chase the things

of this world and cease to acknowledge God—the mistake Israel made.

- **how we speak to those who are rejecting Jesus?** It should compel us to tell others about the gospel. It will give us urgency, determination and compassion for those who aren't yet Christians. It should also remind us just how good the good news of God's grace is, which we have the privilege of sharing.

- **how we feel about the forgiveness we have through Jesus?** As we saw in Study Four, it's only through appreciating the depth of our sin, and the awfulness of the judgment it brings, that we can grasp the wonder of forgiveness. Being forgiven is not just something we understand intellectually; it is something that changes how we *feel*, emotionally. It will give us

great relief and joy; huge gratitude to Jesus; and a deep humility about ourselves.

- **How do people respond to the warning of God's judgment today?** Some listen and repent. Most ignore it; are offended that it is mentioned; excuse their own actions; welcome the idea of judgment, but only for other people.

- **Why do we keep quiet about judgment today?** First, because it's unpopular! At best, we don't like upsetting people; at worst, we don't like losing people's approval. Second, because we often don't really believe in it ourselves. We need Hosea (and God's word) to remind us that it is real.

6 Hosea 11
"NEVER GOING TO GIVE YOU UP"

THE BIG IDEA
God is a holy Judge and our loving Father.

SUMMARY
Hosea has already pictured the relationship between God and Israel as a marriage. Here, the picture changes to that of a parent and child.

God is portrayed as a loving and generous Father, caring for his son Israel, who he called out of slavery in Egypt to be his chosen people. Hosea describes God as teaching Israel (also called Ephraim) to walk (v 3), leading them with bonds of love and

stooping down to feed them, just as a good shepherd would do for his sheep (v 4).

Sadly, despite the love and compassion of God the Father, Israel has turned away from him. As God calls, they have run away (v 2), turned to other gods and forgotten that God was the one who fed and healed them. As a result, God's people face God's right and just punishment for sin. This has been clear throughout the book and is detailed once again here in v 5-7. Because of their refusal to repent and turn back to God, Israel faces attack from Egypt and invasion by Assyria. These verses might seem strange next to the rest of the chapter, but we need to remember that God is both loving and holy. His compassion does not diminish his justice or hatred of sin. Rebellion against God rightly draws his punishment and judgment.

Which makes the next few verses all the more amazing. Despite Israel's sin, God refuses to give them up, but will instead show mercy and compassion. His just and righteous wrath will be turned aside and instead of a lion of judgment (see 5 v 14), God will be the rescuer they will follow in order to be safe and secure.

How all of this can be true is only clear in light of the life and cross of Christ. Jesus is the obedient son that Israel wasn't, and that we cannot be—as Matthew reminds us by quoting from Hosea 11 with reference to the boy Jesus (Matt 2 v 15). So he is able to clothe us with his sonship (Galatians 3 v 26).

Jesus dies the death—takes the punishment—that Israel deserved, and that we deserve. At the cross, God's judgment and mercy meet, rightly punishing sin yet also offering grace and forgiveness to rebellious sinners. This is possible because Jesus is the perfect man, the only one who has obeyed his Father completely, the true Son that Israel could never be.

In a sense, the Christian life is about living as the people we are. In Christ, we are God's sons—no punishment for sin, entirely righteous in our Father's sight. Now we need to live like that!

OPTIONAL EXTRA

Watch part of *The Simpsons* or UK sitcom *My Family* which shows the father interacting with his children in a flawed way. What view of fatherhood is given? Alternatively / in addition, watch *24* Season Seven, episode 24, from 34:25 to 39:25.

Beforehand, explain that the US President, Allison Taylor, has found out that her own daughter is guilty of conspiracy to murder. After watching, ask: What choices could the President have made? What conflict must have been happening in her heart? Was there any way she could be a good President *and* protect her own child from justice? You could show this at the beginning of the session, or after Q9. Draw the comparison between the President and God, who will bring justice for sin, but also longs to forgive his children and protect them from that justice. Unlike the President, he is able to do both, through the cross (Q10).

GUIDANCE FOR QUESTIONS

1. What makes a good father in today's world? This should generate a lot of ideas, both positive and negative, about what it means to be a father as we turn to consider God's fatherhood through Hosea's words. Some people will have very difficult and painful memories associated with their own fathers, or as fathers themselves, and it is important to distinguish between those failings and the perfect fatherhood that God demonstrates.

2. Who does God describe as his "son" here? What is wonderful about God's fatherhood? The nation of Israel is God's "son". These opening verses describe God as a patient, caring, loving father. God has shown love to his child, bringing them out of slavery in Egypt and teaching them to walk, particularly to walk in his ways, and healing their wounds. He has led his son with loving kindness, feeding them and lifting their yoke (which echoes their removal from slavery in Egypt). It is a wonderful picture of God's love, care and kindness to His people.

3. What is desperately sad about the way Israel responds to God's fatherhood? Interwoven in these verses about the fatherly love of God are painful words about Israel's response to God's kindness. Verse 2 tells of God calling to his people, but the more he calls the further they go (something many parents will have experienced). Despite God's love and goodness to them as Father, they turn from him and worship idols—sacrificing to the Baals and man-made images.

4. What do these verses [v 5-7] tell us about God? That he is holy and just. Alongside the love and care of God shown in the first few verses, God is just and holy and cannot tolerate sin. Because of the rebellion of God's people, judgment will fall in the form of the invading army of Assyria. It might seem strange that these words of judgment are placed in the middle of such tender descriptions of God's love, yet we cannot divide God's holiness from his love.

EXPLORE MORE
Read Deuteronomy 29 v 22-28. What difference should these words have made to the way Israel acted? God's judgment in Hosea 11 should not have been a surprise to God's people. They had already been told about the consequences of turning away from God and that his judgment would rightly fall on those who rebel against him and reject his rule. These words formed part of Israel's law and should have determined how they lived and how they treated God. They should have listened!

5. Read Matthew 2 v 13-15. How does Matthew compare Jesus of Nazareth to Israel in Hosea's day? Matthew quotes from Hosea 11 v 1 as he tells how Mary, Joseph and the infant Jesus fled from Herod

to Egypt. In doing so, Matthew is drawing a parallel between Israel in Hosea's day and Jesus. Israel was supposed to act as God's child but chose not to. Jesus, however, was the perfect, obedient Son, responding rightly where Israel failed.

What is he saying about Jesus? In Hosea 11 v 1, Israel is identified as God's "son". Jesus, too, is God's Son, loved by the Father as he lives under his authority. The question as we read the beginning of Matthew is: will Jesus succeed where Israel failed? Will he be an obedient Son? (The answer is in Q6!)

6. Read 1 Peter 2 v 21-23 and Galatians 3 v 26-29. What sort of Son was Jesus? Why is this great news for Christians?
1 Peter 2: He was sinless: he always lived under God the Father's authority. Even when put under extreme pressure, he trusted his Father and lived as God wanted. Jesus is the obedient son of God.
Galatians 3 v 26–29: When we trust in Jesus Christ, we are clothed with him. When God looks at us, he no longer sees our imperfection, but Jesus' perfect obedience. That is wonderfully good news! It means we are "children of God", and will inherit and enjoy all that God gives to his Son Jesus. All that is his, is ours. Christians are "heirs according to the promise"—Hosea 11 v 1-4 describes how God treats Christ, and therefore treats us. Amazing!

7. APPLY: How does this give us hope when we commit the sins of Hosea 11 v 2-4? Though we are sinners as Israel was, believers have been "clothed with Christ"—so our sin is not counted against us. God treats us as though we were Jesus, and therefore perfectly obedient.

• **How does this motivate us to avoid living in these ways?** Several ways:

- Why would we want to live in a way which should bring us God's judgment instead of his fatherly love?
- As we live as Jesus did and Israel didn't, we're able to enjoy life as God's children, and to delight him as our Father.

8. How are things amazingly turned around for Israel here [v 8-11]? Even though his people are determined to turn away from him, God offers forgiveness and mercy. God cannot give up his precious child, and promises that his anger will be turned away. Instead he will show compassion and bring his people back to peace and safety.

- **Read 5 v 14 and 7 v 11. How are God and Israel described here? How does this underline the remarkable turnaround of 11 v 8-11?** 5 v 14 spoke of God as a terrible lion, but now that lion will roar to gather his people once more; 7 v 11 described Israel as a foolish dove looking to other nations for security, but now they will come back from the nations to nest in God's land.

9. What causes this amazing turn of events? God's love. Nothing has changed in the people between verses 7 and 8—Israel has not become more righteous or more obedient. God chooses to be gracious and merciful simply and only because of his loving commitment to his people and the covenant he made with them. He will not give up on his people.

- **In Hosea 11, we're given a privileged glimpse of the heart of God. What two priorities does he have? How do they seem to be in tension with each other?** To be just—to bring judgment on people

who live in his world but reject him and mistreat people he has made. God will be true to his commitment to ensure justice is done in this world. He is holy (v 9). To be merciful—to forgive his people despite their sin, so that he can continue to love them and bless them. God will be true to his commitment to bless his sinful people. He has compassion (v 8). Clearly, there is a tension here! How can God both judge and bless his people? How can he have perfect justice, and show loving mercy? Move on to Q10…!

10. Read Romans 3 v 21-26. How is it that God can be a just Judge and a forgiving Father to his people? God's promises of mercy and forgiveness in v 8-11 are only achieved by Jesus' work on the cross. God is both loving and holy. He cannot ignore sin or leave it unpunished. Only by Jesus' death in our place can God's justice and mercy both be fulfilled. Romans 3 v 21–26 explains how this can be. It is because Jesus was presented as a "sacrifice of atonement"—a sacrifice that makes us right with God. Jesus, the perfect Son, the obedient man, took the punishment for sin on behalf of God's people. On the cross, God's people were (or person was) punished justly for the sin of God's people. And at the cross, God had mercy on his people because it was Jesus who took what his people deserved—the judgment. At the cross God justly judges sin but also graciously provides forgiveness and mercy.

Take your time on this answer if your group needs to, because it is fundamental to understanding who God is and how we are saved. Other New Testament verses which may help you explain how justice and mercy meet at the cross are 2 Corinthians 5 v 21 and 1 Peter 3 v 18.

11. APPLY: These verses direct us to have a correct view of God and his character. What difference does it make if we think of God as...

- **a loving Father, but not a just Judge?**
God becomes a nice companion, but also compromises his own standards, has no answer to the problems of evil in the world or is indifferent to it, and his word cannot be trusted.

- **a just Judge, but not a loving Father?**
God becomes a terrifying Creator, who we must one day face in judgment without anything to say (which is what we deserve). But he also becomes a God who does not keep his word, because he promised to bless and love his people.

- **a loving Father *and* a just Judge?** This is the God of the Bible. What a wonderful God he is! This is a God we can trust, and love, and enjoy knowing—who we know cares about wrongdoing, to whom we can turn when justice is not seen to be done, and who we can call our Father. He is a God who deserves as well as demands our respect and obedience as well as our love.

12. APPLY: Imagine someone reads Hosea 11 and asks you what it's about. How could you use this passage to explain what Jesus offers through his life and death? In Hosea 11, God is displayed as a loving Father, which is the way we would all like God to be toward us. Yet, we also see that God is a just judge, who will not ignore those who rebel and turn away from him. Although we want to know God's love, we deserve God's punishment. We desire to be assured that those words of hope in v 8–11 apply to us. It is Jesus' life, death and resurrection that make this happen. In Jesus we see the love of God demonstrated vividly in his care and compassion for others. We see the beauty of a truly obedient life. But then Jesus dies, undeservedly. And there we see both God's justice and mercy. Jesus was punished in our place, on our behalf. And so he has taken our punishment, and is able to give us his perfect obedience, and his relationship with his Father God. If we have faith in him, God sees us as his children—verses 1-4 apply to us. Through Jesus, *we* can—totally undeservedly—call our Creator and Judge "Father", and enjoy living as his children.

7 Hosea 12 – 13
"HISTORY REPEATING"

THE BIG IDEA
Only God can truly give us safety and security.

SUMMARY
Hosea 12–13 uses various episodes from Israel's past to illustrate the ways in which God's people have failed to trust him.

The first of these episodes is in 12 v 2-6, which focuses on Jacob. The people of Israel were directly descended from Jacob, whose name was changed by God to Israel after his encounter with an angel. As a man, however, Jacob was crafty and deceptive, pictured by the grasping of his brother Esau's foot when he was born.

Jacob's direction is turned around by God's intervention, through an angel who wrestles with him and through a vision of God at Bethel. Hosea uses this episode to show God's people they should trust in God rather than their own skill and achievements. Even Jacob eventually turned and trusted God for his blessing and security—so should Israel.

The theme of trusting in something other than God runs through these chapters. 12 v 7-8 highlights the danger of wealth, which can lead people astray, thinking that the blessings of wealth show a right relationship with God. 13 v 4 brings us back to Mount Sinai and God's law, reminding the people of how God saved and cared for them. They have taken God's kindness but have ignored him, proudly trusting in themselves. So God's judgment will fall (13 v 9–13) and even their kings, who they falsely put their trust and hope in, will not save them.

Chapter 13 ends with a continued note of judgment, in some of the most horrific terms. But in the middle of this pronouncement of guilt there is a wonderful note of hope and grace. 13 v 14 is a tremendous promise that despite the sin of God's people, God will rescue them. Although they put their trust in things that cannot save, God will save them even from the plagues and destruction of death itself. This promise finds its fulfilment in the person of Jesus Christ, who ransoms us from the power of death by taking that death and punishment in our place.

OPTIONAL EXTRA

Do a brief overview or survey of what the Bible tells us about Jacob. Produce a list of personality traits, maybe like a Facebook-style profile, giving a flavour of Jacob's character and attitude to God. You could split your group into pairs and give them different episodes from Jacob's life to build up a picture of him from. Helpful passages: Genesis 25 v 21-26; 25 v 27-34; 27 v 1-40; 29 v 16-30; 30 v 31-43; 32 v 1-21.

GUIDANCE FOR QUESTIONS

1. What lessons have you learned from your past? Answers could be very trivial or deeply profound! It gives an opportunity to consider how our experiences in the past should inform our actions in the present.

2. Who does Hosea compare Israel to? What does 12 v 3-4a suggest he trusted in to get what he wanted? Hosea refers to various episodes in the life of Jacob, especially his birth (v 3), his struggle with an angel and his vision of God (v 4). Jacob was crafty and cunning, often using deceit to achieve his goals. For much of his life, Jacob trusted in his own strength and ability to get what he wanted. Verse 3 reminds us of his birth, born grasping his brother Esau's heel, struggling for supremacy even in the womb. (Jacob's name literally means "he grasps the heel" which in Hebrew has the sense of "one who deceives".) Even his struggle with the angel appears to start out as a desire to overcome God's messenger through his own skill and power. He trusted himself.

3. What is Israel trusting in for safety and security (v 1b, 7-8, 13 v 2)?
- v 1: treaties with God's enemies, the nearby superpowers of Assyria and Egypt.
- v 7-8: their own wealth, trusting in their own resources and willing to justify dishonesty in order to gain more.
- v 8: riches: Israel thought their wealth was evidence of God's favour and spiritual safety, when in fact their hearts were far from God.
- 13 v 2: false gods who are simply the work of human craftsmen.

EXPLORE MORE

Read Genesis 27 v 1–35. How does this incident illustrate Jacob's character? He is willing to dress up as his brother in order to fool his ageing and blind father. Jacob does so in order to gain his father's blessing, as if he could force God's hand and get the blessings that God promises without obedience to God's rule. Jacob was trusting in his own schemes and ingenuity to get what he wanted instead of trusting in God. **How are God's people acting in the same way in Hosea's time?** In a very similar manner: wanting God's blessing but rejecting his rule; trusting in their own skill and ability rather than in God.

4. What did Jacob end up doing (v 4b)? For most of his life, Jacob trusted in his own skill and ability rather than in God. Yet God directly intervened in his life through a vision at Bethel and an encounter with an angel. Through these events, Jacob saw who God was and sought his favour, wrestling with the angel until he gained the angel's blessing. This incident was a turning point for Jacob, moving him from dependence on his own power to a desire for God's blessing.

- **What will it look like for Israel to learn the lesson Jacob learned (v 6)?** Return to God, trusting not in their own work but God's actions for them ("wait for your God"), and seeking to reflect his character in their lives by showing love and justice.

⌄

- **God is calling Israel to turn their attitude and actions around completely. What would the opposite of their current outlook, as seen in 12 v 1 and 7-8, look like?**

5. APPLY: Where do people today look for safety and security instead of God? What makes these things attractive things to rely on? We have seen how God's people have put their trust in things others than God—themselves, their skill and wealth—and those temptations are still a danger to us today. The same tendency to trust in ourselves, our ability, our career, our achievements or our bank balance, can draw us away from trusting God. These things are attractive because they are what the world chases and what we are constantly told makes life worth living; because our hearts naturally want to shut God out and find other things to love and serve; and because they all allow us to "save" ourselves—to gain life through our own efforts. We love to be our own saviours, because it means we can feel that we are in control; and because it means we don't have to humbly accept that we're not God, and can't give ourselves what we need.

6. Which events from Israel's past are highlighted here (v 4-5, 10)? What do they tell us about God and his people? Note: You might want to point your group to these verses (split your group into pairs to speed it up): Exodus 3 v 8; 20 v 3; 16 v 2-4; 1 Samuel 8 v 4-7.

- The events of the Exodus, as well as the giving of the Law at Mount Sinai with the repetition of the first of the Ten Commandments in verse 4.
- Verse 10 recalls how God's people asked for a king like the nations around them, rejecting God as their king and ruler. They highlight God's care and compassion (v 5) as well as his holiness and rule (v 9).

Once again, we see God's people rejecting God as their king and provider and being overcome by pride instead (v 6).

EXPLORE MORE

Read 1 Samuel 8 v 1–8 . Why do the people ask for a king? What is wrong with their request and how does it show the state of their hearts? 1 Samuel chapter 8 tells how the elders of Israel asked Samuel to give them a king to lead them when he died. At first glance this seems like a good thing, motivated by the ungodly behaviour of Samuel's sons. However, their words reveal another motive in their request: they want a king "such as all the other nations have". It's a desire to be like other nations. It is also a rejection of God as their King and Ruler (v 7).

How is the same attitude at work in Hosea's day? They too looked to their king and princes to save them and keep them safe, and to other nations for their model (12 v 1), rather than looking to God for safety and security.

7. How do verses 5-6 and 9-11 show us where Israel was looking for security: and why they were foolish to do so?

- *v 5-6:* They are trusting in themselves. Yet God was the One who cared for them in the desert, as he brought them out of slavery in Egypt, providing Israel with food, water and protection. It wasn't Israel who did this for themselves: yet now they have forgotten God and rely on themselves.
- *v 9-11:* Kings and princes, like the nations around them; despite the fact that the God of creation offered to be their helper.

8. What powerful pictures are used to describe God's judgment?

- v 7-8: A series of wild animals, powerful and ferocious, as dangerous as a mother who has been robbed of her children.
- v 10: A people without the rulers they had trusted in.
- v 13: Israel will be like a clueless unborn

child. They will know great pain, but it will not do any good—nothing will come of it because they won't respond by returning to God (the wise thing to do).

9. Why does verse 14 seem out of place in this passage? In the middle of stark words about the people's sin and God's judgment, he promises to rescue his people, so that not only will they be saved from their earthly enemies, but they will also be delivered from death, the greatest enemy. It is amazing grace, as Israel have not done anything to deserve such mercy.

- **What can God do that neither idols (v 1) nor kings (v 10) can?** He can conquer death and save them from the grave. No idol, king, prince, nation or power can do that: only God can!

10. Read 1 Corinthians 15 v 20-21, 51-58. How does God achieve the promise of Hosea 13 v 14? The "sting of death" is sin, which each one of us has committed, and so we face God's judgment. The victory over sin and death, however, has been won through the Lord Jesus Christ. In his life he obeyed the law, so sin had no power over him (v 56). And so death had no power over him, either—God raised him from the dead. And so in him we can have forgiveness of sins and be raised from the dead ourselves (v 21). Victory and life are given to anyone who trusts in Jesus as Lord (v 58). Although we do not see the full reality of this defeat of death yet, we look forward to that day when Jesus returns and death is done away with for good (v 54).

11. APPLY: Why can Jesus give us true safety and security? Because he has conquered death. He has removed our greatest enemy, death—the one which makes a mockery of all other things we trust in to give us real, lasting life. And beyond death, he will give us immortal, imperishable, perfect bodies (eternal life for Jesus' people is a physical existence, in this—perfected—world). Since his resurrection shows and proves he has defeated our invincible enemy, we can trust Jesus in the difficulties and struggles of life now.

12. APPLY: How should we respond to the defeat of death (1 Corinthians 15 v 58)? First, we should stand firm, not moved from our trust in Jesus in every aspect of our lives. Second, we should give ourselves fully to the work of the Lord,

because only this work lasts for eternity. We may achieve good, even great, things in other areas of our life, but only what we do for God is not in vain.

• **What will this look like in our everyday lives?** For some, this means going to work in the mission field. For all of us, it means doing everything for God's glory. Think of specific ways in which your group has the opportunity to be part of "the work of the Lord".

• **APPLY: How might we do the Lord's work, but not give ourselves fully to it? Why do we often hold back?**

8 Hosea 14
"RETURN TO ME"

THE BIG IDEA
God lavishes his grace and blessing on those who turn back to him.

SUMMARY
The theme of chapter 14 is summed up in the command of the first verse: "Return, Israel, to the LORD your God". In fact, this theme of returning to God has run through the whole book, illustrated in Hosea taking back Gomer, his unfaithful wife, and urged time and time again as the prophet has told Israel of their sin.

Israel desperately needs to return to the LORD because of their sinfulness and rebellion against him. They have gone astray by trusting in other things: their military might, and that of the neighbouring superpower

Assyria, and the gods that their own hands have made (v 3). Israel is urged to turn away from this idolatry, turn back to God and ask for his forgiveness.

The method of their return is spelled out in verse 2: "Take words with you … Say to him…". At first this might seem odd, especially since Israel has been rebuked for paying lip-service to God back in chapter 6. But the repentance here is to be heartfelt and genuine, based on a true knowledge of God and his character—his goodness, mercy, holiness—and turning away from sinful behaviour.

God's response to real repentance is seen in verses 4-8. His grace will provide healing and love for a wayward people, and his anger will turn away. Hosea gives wonderful

pictures of God's goodness to his people—
a thriving plant and a fruitful tree. A life
with God delivers not only salvation, but
also great blessing in life.

The last verse is, like the whole of the book,
a challenge to Israel in Hosea's day, and to
us who read it today. Will we be wise and
discerning as we hear Hosea's exposure
of our sin and idolatry? Will we return to
the Lord and walk in his ways? Or will we
stumble in sin? Israel stumbled instead of
returning, and were invaded by Assyria in
722 BC (see the second Explore More). Will
we follow their example or put our trust in
the God who shows mercy and compassion
to those who return to him?

OPTIONAL EXTRA

If you have a keen gardener in your group,
ask them to speak for a few minutes about
why they love growing things; what they
do for the bushes/trees in their garden;
and what makes a healthy (or "happy")
tree. This links into the image of growing,
healthy, fruitful trees that Hosea uses to
describe the people of God (v 5-8).

GUIDANCE FOR QUESTIONS

**1. What would society say makes
someone wise?** Wisdom is a quality often
undervalued in contemporary society. Where
it is portrayed, perhaps in books or films, it
is often reduced to being the same as old
or cautious or experienced. Alternatively,
wisdom can be associated with academics
and being "bookish"—knowing a lot about
a particular subject. God, through Hosea,
will give us a very different picture of what
wisdom is all about.

- **Would you personally add or change
  anything in that definition?** Don't allow
  this discussion to go on too long!

**2. What does God tell Israel to do,
and why (v 1)?** Return to the Lord, to an
obedient covenant relationship with him.
They need to do this because they have
sinned, and this has been their downfall—it
has left them not enjoying the life they could
have had with God as their Ruler.

- **Think back to what we have seen
  of Israel in Hosea's day. Why is it
  amazing that they have the option
  of doing verse 1?** Time and time again
  throughout Hosea we have seen how
  God's people have rebelled against him,
  rejecting his commands. Yet despite their
  persistent sin and idolatry, he is holding
  out the offer of return and blessing.

3. How are Israel to return (v 2-3)?
"Take words with you" ie: speak to God.
The words they are to use are important—
asking for God's forgiveness, confessing
their sin and idolatry, recalling God's
character and asking for his grace and
strength to live changed lives.

- **What does returning to the Lord mean
  turning away from?** Things that are not
  God. In these verses two particular areas
  are highlighted: trust in military might
  and trust in idols. The people of Israel
  were depending on their own armies as
  well as the army of Assyria (a nation who
  would soon invade Israel). They also put
  their trust in idols, gods that their own
  hands had made instead of the true God,
  who can show them compassion. Truly
  returning to the Lord will mean turning
  away from these things—accepting that
  they cannot provide security or salvation.

- **Read 6 v 1-4. How is the return God
  calls for in chapter 14 different from
  the one he rejected in chapter 6?** Back
  in Hosea 6 v 1-4, the people were rebuked
  by God because of the words they used.

At that point they only paid lip-service to the idea of returning to God. Here they are to use words, but accompany them with a *changed attitude of heart*. In chapter 6, there was no acknowledgement of their sin. In chapter 14, however, there is a genuine desire for God's mercy, flowing from a heartfelt recognition of the people's idolatry and rejection of God.

EXPLORE MORE
Read Hebrews 13 v 15-16 and James 3 v 9-12. What does it mean for Christians to "offer the fruit of our lips"?
Hebrews 13: It involves both praise of God and confession of Jesus' name: being willing to speak up for Jesus and be known as his follower.
James 3: Our lips reflect the state of our hearts. Someone who praises God for his mercy and grace cannot use those same lips to utter curses and improper talk.
As Christians, we should be careful about the words we use, with our speech being distinctive and matching our status as people saved by God.

4. APPLY: How can people return to, and stay in, a relationship with God?
Returning to a relationship with God means turning from things that are wrong, and turning back to God. All that is required to turn back to God is to ask for his forgiveness, acknowledging our sinfulness and coming to him in prayer. However, although all we need are words to return, the genuineness of those words will be shown in changed attitude, direction and actions in our lives.
And we go on as we started. Israel had been God's people for centuries, loved by him; yet they were still sinful, still needed forgiveness, and so still needed to repent. As the German Reformer Martin Luther once said, the

Christian is always sinful, always repentant, and always justified, or forgiven.

5. What is life like for people who turn back to God? Wonderful!
- *v 4:* God will turn aside his judgment and love his people freely, healing their waywardness and rebellion. By asking for his forgiveness, God's people can experience the lavish grace and mercy of God.
- *v 5-8:* This is a vivid illustration of the abundance of God's goodness. Hosea describes God as being water and life to his people, making them like a beautiful flower which blossoms, or a cedar of Lebanon, which, as the tallest tree of those times, was an image of strength and security. They will be a plant which flourishes and bears much fruit, like a healthy olive tree, a grape-producing vine or a vast tree that people can shelter under.

6. Where does Israel's fruitfulness come from? How will they continue to be fruitful in the future?
In the middle of this picture of fruitfulness, it is important to remember that it is *God* who brings this fruit. He is the one who provides Israel with their nourishment (v 5) and tells his people "your fruitfulness comes from me" (v 8). In order to continue to bear fruit and prosper, Israel must continue to depend on God, finding their provision and security in him.
Note: It is worth pointing out that these verses remind us that life with God, under his rule, is better than life without him, trusting in ourselves or other things. The Christian life is not about giving up a fulfilling life now as the price for being given eternal life: it is about enjoying life as God designed it now, and knowing this will continue into eternity.

7. How does the beginning of v 8 interrupt the general tone of this chapter? Why does God say this here, do you think? In the middle of these wonderful promises of God, there is a clear warning. There is a real danger that Israel (called Ephraim here) will continue to trust in idols instead of God. Verse 8 warns God's people how utterly ludicrous that would be. God will not tolerate his people worshipping him *and* idols; Israel must choose one or the other. Great blessing is on offer, but not if the people choose to continue to be unfaithful to the God who gives blessing.

8. APPLY: How could you use v 1-8 to explain to a non-Christian what becoming a Christian, and being a Christian, is about? Many people think being a Christian is about being religious enough or doing good deeds to others. Hosea 14 shows us that far from being good enough, becoming a Christian means recognising that we have turned away from God and are in desperate danger—we face his deserved judgment. All we can do is accept God's offer of rescue and ask for His forgiveness, made possible through Jesus' death and resurrection. We can then experience God's generous blessing, which is pictured in these verses, not because of our effort but only because of God's goodness.

- **Imagine you have a friend who has been living as a Christian, but who has now turned their back on God. How could you use these verses to encourage and challenge them?** God wants them to return to him. He was willing to forgive Israel, despite all they'd done—he is willing to forgive your friend. They need to realise that they've been worshipping something else, and turn from it. Life with God is wonderful.

Whatever it is they're living for, it's not going to deliver what they hoped for; and it cannot give them the blessing that God offers. They can simply speak to God, with their lips and in their heart, turning back to him, and he'll forgive and bless them.

9. What does it mean to be wise? A truly wise person is not necessarily someone who has lived a long time or studied intensely. Rather a wise person pays attention to what God says and walks in the ways of the Lord. True wisdom is to listen to God and put his word into practice (see Matthew 7 v 24-27). **What is the other option given here?** The alternative is to reject what God has said, continuing in stubborn rebellion and refusing to return. The result for those who follow this path is that they will stumble, which will be their downfall ("stumble" in v 9 and "downfall" in v 1 are the same word).

EXPLORE MORE
Read 2 Kings 17 v 7-20. How do you see the warnings from Hosea echoed in these verses? Israel was facing ruin because of their unfaithfulness: idolatry and worship of other gods, breaking the covenant, and becoming like the nations around them. **What option from Hosea 14 v 9 did Israel choose? With what result?** Sadly, Israel chose to ignore God and his words, continuing in their idolatry and rejection of God's truth. The end result was that the northern kingdom of Israel was invaded by Assyria (the superpower whose alliance Israel had trusted in for security) in 722 BC, and the verdict of 2 Kings is that "the Lord rejected all the people of Israel … he thrust them from his presence."

10. APPLY: Read John 15 v 5-8. How should we live as wise and fruitful Christians? Jesus uses Hosea's image of a fruitful vine to describe his relationship with his followers. God's desire for all who trust Jesus is for them to bear fruit—the evidence of a life touched by God's grace. To bear fruit, Jesus' disciples must "remain" in him: continue to trust him, listen to his words and depend on him in prayer (15 v 7).

11. APPLY: Think back over the book of Hosea as a whole. These questions are an opportunity for you to review the book as a whole, and think through how it has changed your group's appreciation of who God is, and given them a desire (and knowledge) to live his way. If you have time, have fun summing Hosea up in fewer and fewer words, till you get to two or three!

thegoodbook
COMPANY
Opening up the Bible

At The Good Book Company, we are dedicated to helping Christians and local churches grow. We believe that God's growth process always starts with hearing clearly what he has said to us through his timeless word—the Bible.

Ever since we opened our doors in 1991, we have been striving to produce resources that honour God in the way the Bible is used. We have grown to become an international provider of user-friendly resources to the Christian community, with believers of all backgrounds and denominations using our Bible studies, books, evangelistic resources, DVD-based courses and training events.

We want to equip ordinary Christians to live for Christ day by day, and churches to grow in their knowledge of God, their love for one another, and the effectiveness of their outreach.

Call us for a discussion of your needs or visit one of our local websites for more information on the resources and services we provide.

Your friends at The Good Book Company

UK & EUROPE   thegoodbook.co.uk   0333 123 0880
NORTH AMERICA   thegoodbook.com   866 244 2165
AUSTRALIA   thegoodbook.com.au   (02) 6100 4211
NEW ZEALAND   thegoodbook.co.nz   (+64) 3 343 2463

  WWW.CHRISTIANITYEXPLORED.ORG
Our partner site is a great place for those exploring the Christian faith, with a clear explanation of the good news, powerful testimonies and answers to difficult questions.